Because ORGAN of DONATION

Pediatric Stories

Collected by
BRENDA E. CORTEZ

Because of Organ Donation – Pediatric Stories
Foreword: Susan Angel Miller and Sara Miller
Contributing Editors: Brenda E. Cortez, Jean Sime
Contributing Authors: Kelli Bartleson, Kristen Cowan,
Jamie Porter, Stephanie Skrede, Kayla Fink, Beth Battista,
Stephanie Mullett, John Welch, Dan Richardson, Riki Graves,
Gail Burant, Harmony Wells, Jen Lau, Rachel Rodriguez,
Tom Schaefer, Sara Snider, Patti DiSanto
Cover Design: Tabassum Hashmi
Interior Layout: Michael Nicloy

All images have been provided by the individual contributors.
Front Cover Photo: Lucy Munrayos, Punta Gorda, Florida

ISBN: 979-8-9881723-0-7

Published by BC Books, LLC, Franklin, Wisconsin
Quantity order requests may be emailed to the Publisher:
info@bcbooksllc.com

BC BOOKS, LLC

This book is dedicated to every child and family who has ever been touched by organ donation or transplant. You are stronger and braver than you know. May God bless you and shine His light on you each and every day.

To all the angel heroes who will never get to be an adult on this earth, I pray that you are singing and dancing in the heavens as you watch down and protect your earthly family. Jesus loves you, this I know.

"Be an Organ Donor and Help Others With Love"

Brenda E. Cortez

Table of Contents

Foreword

By Susan Angel Miller,
and Sara Miller

On the same day my fourteen-year-old daughter was declared legally brain-dead, my husband and I were asked a question no parent wants to answer.

We were asked to donate Laura's organs. We did not know what to do. We had always believed organ donation to be a generous and noble concept, but never a practical, time-sensitive, and emotional decision we would have to make on behalf of our oldest, precious daughter. Laura had not even been old enough to declare her organ donation wishes on her driver's license, and we had never talked about the subject.

We turned to our rabbi who had been sitting quietly in the corner of the hospital family waiting room. When he told us that Judaism believes that saving a life is the highest mitzvah, we were comforted. When our twelve-year-old middle daughter joined the conversation and pleaded with us to allow Laura's organs to save someone else's life, we were convinced. We said yes with the fervent hope of sparing another family the pain and despair we were suffering.

This decision, made on the worst day of our lives, ignited a light that grows brighter as the years pass.

Whether it is connecting with generous living donors like Brenda, or reading and listening to the experiences of recipients and donor families like ours, these stories give us and others hope. They dispel myths. They change hearts and minds.

Stories, like the ones in this book, educate readers about the fragility and preciousness of life. They inspire personal conversations about organ donation wishes and increased registrations, and ultimately, more lives are saved and healed.

These stories reveal profoundly personal moments and a rare perspective into the heartache of donor families, the relief and joy of the recipients, and the gratitude and awe of all.

Susan Angel Miller
Donor Mom
Author of *Permission to Thrive: My Journey from Grief to Growth*

In the aftermath of my sister's sudden death from a brain tumor, I found myself sharing her story to her peers. I explained her medical condition, talked about the care she received in the hospital, and communicated the despair our family was feeling. I could feel people's sadness and disbelief.

When I shared that my sister, Laura, was an organ donor who saved the life of a forty-year-old special education teacher in New York, this sadness and disbelief changed into awe and curiosity.

What is organ donation? How does it work? Why doesn't everyone donate their organs?

I became passionate about sharing my sister's story, and in the process, learned how many others have powerful stories that change hearts and minds. That's what inspired me to found SODA: Student Organ Donation Advocates in 2014, which has grown to over fifty SODA chapters that educate with the purpose of saving and healing lives. I am thrilled and honored to contribute to this compelling compilation of stories, because I am certain of their profound, life-changing impact.

Sara Miller
Founder and President of SODA: Student Organ Donation Advocates

Introduction

By Brenda E. Cortez

More Than 1,700 Children Received Life-Saving Transplants in 2020

Organ donation and transplantation is scary as an adult, but for a child or the parent of a child, it is the unthinkable. Children from birth to age seventeen make up almost 3% of the more than 100,000 people on the national transplant waiting list. Since I have been advocating for organ donation awareness, this number has gone down, but we still have so much work to do. Every day, nine people die while waiting for their life-saving organ, which is nine too many. No person deserves to die waiting for the gift of life. Not ever.

When I donated one of my kidneys eighteen years ago to another mom, I did not know anything about living donation, but I knew I needed to help that mom. I have often wished I had another kidney, or multiple kidneys, to donate, especially to a child. Many other living donors I've met or talked with have shared these same thoughts.

In our first *Because of Organ Donation* book, you read about many living donors, and I am happy to say you will in this book too: not only living kidney donors, but also living liver donors. Donating a portion of your liver is a much more involved surgery than donating a kidney, so I personally extend my highest gratitude to these amazing people. After I wrote the *Howl Loves His New Liver* book, I learned there were many more pediatric liver transplants than I had imagined, and that is because of a liver disease called biliary atresia (BA). BA is a rare disease of the liver and bile ducts that affects infants. In this book, you will learn why transplant is so important for babies affected by BA. Organ failure can affect any main organ in both adults and children. Just like in book one, you will read about some amazing little heart warriors in this book.

All organ donors are heroes, both living and deceased. But, in my humble opinion, the families of babies and children who make the decision for their child to save other lives, so another family doesn't have to experience the immense pain and loss that they themselves are experiencing, are the truly amazing heroes. You will read about some of these little ones and their families in the coming chapters. I ask that you pray for them, or send love and light their way, because no matter how much time has passed since the loss of their child, the pain is still raw and real. I know that the opportunity for their precious loved one to live on in others is what helps them survive the tragedy they have been through.

Organ donation can save lives, and age does not discriminate. We need to continue to share stories like these so people know the impact that being an organ donor can make. We need to keep raising awareness and reduce the wait time for a life-saving organ. Because of organ donation, someone whose life ended too soon can fulfill a purpose they may never have realized they would be capable of.

Brenda E. Cortez
Living Donor, Author, Publisher
www.brendacortez.com

Jaylee Strong

By Kelli Bartleson

I glanced over to see a resuscitator bag secured to our new baby's face. "Is she ok?" I yelled, just seconds after our new bundle of joy had entered the world. Jaylee was born July 3rd, 2018—our (almost) firecracker baby. We did not find out her gender before she was born because we wanted to be surprised. Oh my, did she give us plenty of surprises. Our baby girl gave us many amazing surprises, in addition to plenty of scary ones …

Jaylee was petite at birth, but otherwise deemed healthy. She was kept in the Neonatal Intensive Care Unit (NICU) the first night, so she could be monitored closely and to make sure she was thriving. My husband, Brandon, met Jaylee in the NICU, and me shortly after. Seeing her for the first time was truly love at first sight. It amazed me how something so tiny could inspire a love so huge. Jaylee overcame a few more initial obstacles, which included a grade one brain bleed. Because of the brain bleed, our daughter was transported to a NICU at a bigger hospital, one that was better equipped to deal with any issues should they arise. Jaylee was in that NICU for one week. Her brain bleed eventually resolved itself, and her medical team had no other concerns, so she was healthy enough to go home on July 11th, 2018.

When we arrived home, life was perfect with our daughter. Just to say the word "daughter" felt surreal and gave me goose bumps.

Life went on as expected with a baby. Our days were short, the nights were long; Jaylee started daycare, and Brandon and I both worked. We were living a life we had created and loved. As to be expected, Jaylee caught various colds and viruses at daycare. But virus after virus … emergency room visits, hospital stays, pneumonia, urinary tract infections, ear infections … turned into our worst nightmare. While most infants recover and feel well after some time, Jaylee became sicker and more lethargic. Brandon and I became louder, voicing our concerns about our new baby. After irregular bloodwork at the beginning of December 2018, we ended up at Blank Children's Hospital to rule out a scary word: *leukemia*. After a full day's worth of visits and blood tests, whatever it was didn't appear to be a leukemia diagnosis. But, still, I needed more answers. My gut was telling me something was wrong.

On January 31st, 2019, Jaylee woke up not feeling well. She was vomiting, pale, and weak and seemed like she was in pain. She wasn't acting well or appearing well. My gut instinct was to pick up the phone and call 911, and that is exactly what I did. After an ambulance ride, we arrived at the emergency room (ER). Several tests, including a respiratory panel and a chest X-ray, were done. We were told, once again, that everything looked good, and we were sent home with a bad gut feeling and no answers. The next morning, February 1st, 2019, my phone rang early. It was a doctor from Jaylee's primary care clinic.

He said, "I saw in Jaylee's chart this morning that she had an ER visit last night. I would like you to come in this morning to repeat her chest X-ray."

Brandon and I didn't know what to think, and we were nervous that they wanted her back right away. We arrived at the clinic and met with the doctor. He explained when he looked at the chest X-ray from last night, he had noticed her lungs looked good, but her heart looked enlarged. He wanted us to see a pediatric cardiologist in a nearby bigger city, so Jaylee could have an echo (heart ultrasound) done. Fear immediately ran through my entire body. I was trying to remain calm, but now we were worried about our daughter's heart.

We arrived at Mercy Pediatric Cardiology, and they performed the echo. The doctor then came in, and our world started spiraling. Words suddenly didn't make sense. I felt numb. They told us that Jaylee's left ventricle wasn't working like it should, and that her heart was failing. She needed to get somewhere that could treat her as soon as possible. A normal heart function has an ejection fraction (EF) of 55%–75%, and Jaylee's was at 11%. They diagnosed her with cardiomyopathy. It felt like a nightmare, like we were living someone else's life …

When we arrived in Iowa City, Jaylee was strapped down in her car seat on a stretcher. She went straight up to the Pediatric Intensive Care Unit (PICU), and they told us we needed to go to the waiting room while they placed a PICC line in her. Essentially, this is a large IV that runs straight to a main artery with medication to help her heart function improve right away. The goal that first night was to keep her comfortable, give her the medication she needed, and run numerous tests.

For a few days and through many tests, Jaylee was kept stable while they tried to figure out the cause of her failing heart, as well as the next move to give her the best chance of survival. I kept thinking, *When I hear the words "heart failure," I don't think of a 6-month-old baby*. I didn't even know that a heart failure pediatric doctor even existed, and I had no clue what was going to fix Jaylee's broken heart. I thought I was supposed to fix everything because I'm her mom and that's what moms do. We fix boo-boos and make our babies feel better.

This was such a stressful and scary time for Brandon and me. Between talking with the doctors and trying to soothe Jaylee by talking or singing to her, trying to make time for us was an immense challenge. We had to remind ourselves that we had to eat and sleep since it felt like all the days were running together. Every little ding of a machine would send both of us flying out of bed. It hit us like a ton of bricks when one doctor told us that our daughter was one of the sickest kids in the state. The scariest part about undetected heart defects and diseases is that children can disguise illnesses so well; they look typical on the outside, but on the inside, they are fighting a huge battle. Jaylee had a CT scan to try and determine if it was a virus that had attacked her heart, but it didn't look to be that way. The medical team was thinking it was most likely genetics, that something she was born with had caused this. Medications weren't working miraculously like we had hoped for, either. They were improving her heart function ever so slightly, but not enough.

Since nothing else was working, the next plan of action was a surgery to attach Jaylee's heart to a Left Ventricular Assistant Device (LVAD), which would assist her heart while allowing her to grow. The LVAD would help her feel better so she could do typical baby things, and it would also help all her organs thrive. I kept asking the doctors, "What is going to heal my baby?" They told us that medications could help, and that the LVAD might heal her heart by giving it the rest it needs. The worst-case scenario was that she would need a heart transplant. Eventually, we learned that was exactly what Jaylee needed to heal. Our daughter needed a new heart to be a typical child again, to have a chance to survive and thrive.

Jaylee was added to the transplant list on February 7th, 2019. We signed consent forms and read the letter that was written by her transplant team to the United Network for Organ Sharing (UNOS) to add Jaylee to the transplant list. We had many educational meetings, financial meetings, and emotional support visits. To hear the words "Your daughter needs a new heart" just didn't seem real or even possible at all. Never did we think taking Jaylee in for a simple virus would turn into the need for a heart transplant.

The heart failure doctor came in one afternoon when we were having an emotionally tough day. He looked at Brandon and me and said, "I know one thing: You have made an incredibly strong baby."

He was right. Jaylee is a fighter, and she had shown us how strong she was, so we came up with the term *Jaylee Strong*. Our community gathered to support us and Jaylee, and they gave us so much more support than we ever could have expected. We weren't in this alone anymore. At this point, we knew what we were praying for. As much as we didn't like what it ultimately meant, and as strange as it was the first time, I prayed for my baby to receive a new heart. I felt a sense of relief knowing what she needed to survive. I wrote in a journal each day we were in the hospital, and one day I wrote, "I would gladly take your place, Jaylee. If I could donate my heart to you, believe me, I would." The wait continued, and we prayed nonstop for a new heart.

A few more days went by, but to us, a few days seemed like a lifetime. Jaylee continued to show us what a fighter she was. But the unknowns and the "what if" thoughts that would sneak up were the most painful. However, Jaylee continued to prove that sometimes the smallest people can put up the biggest fight. Neither Brandon nor I left Jaylee's side the entire time. We took it day by day, hour by hour, minute by minute. At this point, her EF still didn't seem to be improving, so the LVAD surgery was a go. The LVAD's purpose was to bridge the gap until she would receive a new heart. I had several dreams while we were in the hospital. I dreamt we were home as a family of three and things were back to normal, but then I would wake up and be hit with reality. The harder I pinched myself, the more real it became. Jaylee's LVAD surgery was scheduled for the next morning, so the night before I wrote to Jaylee in my journal. "Dear Jaylee, you have given me a purpose, and you have shown Daddy and me what true love is." My words were true; our daughter had shown us the kind of love that hurts. The day Jaylee was born, we met the love of our lives.

Jaylee's first open heart surgery took place on February 11th, 2019. Brandon and I found it very difficult to sleep the night before, as I'm sure any parent would. Before they took her back to the operating room (OR), we both got to hold her for the first time in a week. The surgery took a total of four hours, and we received periodic updates from the nurse in the OR. We had tons of family at the hospital with us, and we all tried to stay busy in the waiting room to keep our minds from wandering toward those "what if" thoughts. Then we saw a bed surrounded by doctors, surgeons, nurses, beeps, and buzzers exit the OR. It was Jaylee. They took her into her room and hooked her up on every monitor imaginable, and then we finally got to see our baby.

The surgeon came to talk with us and let us know she had done amazing. He seemed a little surprised but said everything had gone very smoothly. Her heart behaved with the sedation, and she handled everything very well. Jaylee was on a paralytic, lots of pain medication, and was intubated. Her eyes had a goop-like glue substance over them to help keep them healthy, since they would be closed for so long and could become too dry. I couldn't wait for the day I could see her pretty eyes again and we would be one step closer to being home together. Jaylee was a true warrior, and she now had a long zipper scar down her chest to prove it.

It was hard to get used to seeing the LVAD connected to Jaylee, but we both had a gift of looking past all the wires and cannulas to see just Jaylee. A week went by with great progress as she recovered. There was always a fine balance between keeping her blood thinned to prevent clots, but thick enough so she didn't bleed. Her eyes had started opening a bit, and you could tell she was hearing our voices. Jaylee continued to improve, and therapists started visiting her. Her favorite time of the day was music therapy. However, living inpatient became hard; it tested us mentally, emotionally, and physically. It was a very sad floor to live on. We saw many children life-flighted in, and some passed away. Witnessing that daily was hard, but we made the most of our life in the hospital with Jaylee. We stayed positive as best as we could, and we grew close to the nurses and staff. They became family to us—a shoulder to cry on in the middle of the night when Jaylee ran into complications, and they celebrated each milestone with us. Eventually, Jaylee began moving her arms and legs more and would reach out for us. It was finally time for her to be extubated. She was breathing on her own after her first open heart surgery!

After weeks of waiting, we were able to finally hold our daughter. Her sweet personality was shining through, and she was acting more like herself with little laughs and smiles. Another month passed as we continued to wait, living life in the hospital. We kept our positive outlook, and despite some setbacks, Jaylee made many big strides forward. Brandon and I became involved with support groups and organizations that had families in similar situations. It was nice to meet up with other parents and share stories we could relate to. It made us realize that we really weren't alone. It was crazy how time flew by, and yet the days ran together, making it seem like time was standing still. Jaylee began practicing her eating skills and had lots of therapy sessions. She also played, jammed to music, had dress-up days, and took countless wagon rides. We took many pictures! It was so nice to see her resume normal baby activities. We were starting to feel somewhat alive again. Soon, Jaylee was eight months old! We celebrated every milestone, big or small, continuing to make the best of each day.

Jaylee's genetic tests finally came back at the end of March, and the results explained what had caused her cardiomyopathy. The results showed that Jaylee had a deletion on one of her chromosomes —chromosome 7. This deletion can come with a variety of complications, the worst of which is developing cardiomyopathy. Since the study of genetics in these cases is so new, doctors today still don't know what else this means for Jaylee, so we continue to watch and see how she develops, just like all parents do. As the genetics doctor said, "Don't obsess over these results. Let's focus on getting her a new heart and see what Jaylee does." We moved forward and dealt with any challenges as they arose. Many times, I couldn't help but feel how unfair the situation was. Jaylee didn't deserve this, and honestly, at times I have asked myself the question "Why her?" But we continued to learn and become stronger as a team, while striving to be the best parents for Jaylee. She deserves it, and she deserves to be loved and to thrive the best that she can.

We dealt with some more bumps in the road; we ended up finding a cyst-like mass under Jaylee's incision. The medical team removed it, but it didn't want to stop bleeding, so this led to a blood transfusion. Eventually, it had to be cauterized to help stop the bleeding. The positives were that it wasn't infected, and she overcame that obstacle in true Jaylee fashion—like a warrior. During this time, Jaylee began trying to sit up and was becoming more interactive. It amazed me how much strength and weight she had gained from being on the LVAD. It truly saved her life. Soon her hair started growing, her teeth started popping through, and she was gaining some impressive cheeks! We continued to wait, and Jaylee waited with the LVAD for a total of 73 days …

On April 25th, 2019, the day we had been waiting and praying for finally came. WE GOT THE CALL! This is the day that saved Jaylee's life; it was the beginning of a new start for her, and a second chance at life. However, when we had woken up that morning, it was just another typical day in the hospital. We were watching a movie while I was rocking Jaylee in a chair. I heard a knock on our door, and it was Jaylee's nurse for that day, asking if the doctor could come in to speak with us. I felt my heart sink. Jaylee's doctor came in and told us that there was a potential donor, and her transplant surgery was looking to be tomorrow early morning. There would be lots of pokes and tests that evening, and they would prep Jaylee for surgery the next day. All of that didn't matter because she was getting a new heart! The evening was long, with lots of emotions and very little sleep. Everything was lined up and looked like a go for early the next morning. We called family; some arrived that night to be with us and Jaylee, and many arrived the next morning before her surgery.

There were lots of tears of relief and joy, but there were also tears of sorrow for the donor family. The amazing joy we had knowing

Jaylee was receiving a life-saving heart transplant also hit us strangely, because we knew another family was grieving over the loss of their child. It was a strange thought to know another child had to die in order for ours to live. A part of us felt a form of survivor's guilt. However, we were reassured by many that what happened to this child was going to happen regardless of what Jaylee needed, and hearing that helped ease some of those thoughts.

April 26th, 2019—the day had come. It was go time. We all prayed and gave Jaylee so many hugs. All of us were ready for this day. It had been a long time coming, and our daughter deserved a second chance at life. Brandon and I walked Jaylee to the operating room doors at 7:30 AM, past all the family, friends, doctors, nurses, and staff that had supported us throughout this journey. They all cried tears of happiness along with us. We gave Jaylee more hugs, and I whispered in her ear, "You've got this! I love you more than life." In the elevator on the way to the OR, the anesthesiologist said, "How she is laying tells me surgery will go well." Brandon and I were confused by that statement. Jaylee was lying with one arm up over her head and her ankle was resting on the opposite knee, looking very chill, calm, and confident. The anesthesiologist said he was once told that when a patient goes into the OR in that exact pose, it is good luck. As we walked away, we felt a sense of relief and also numbness. While I felt strong, I also felt as if I could have collapsed.

Time dragged on as we waited for news during the surgery. We were finally updated that Jaylee was taken off bypass around 1:00 PM and her new heart was pumping in her body on its own! The new heart was a little sluggish and stiff at first, but the function improved and was working great! They did have to do some pacing to help her heart with some arrhythmia issues. Then, after seven long hours, her surgeon came into the waiting room to tell us her surgery was done, her heart was doing well, and we would be able to see her soon. When we were able to see Jaylee, I noticed she was pink and had a strong pulse, but she was very swollen. She was hooked up to a lot of machines, and I knew she had a long road ahead of her. But I knew Jaylee could do it—we would do it together. We were told that the first 24-48 hours were very crucial, and they had to watch her very carefully in case any complications should arise.

Around 10:30 PM, they asked us to make our way to the conference room. I headed to Jaylee's room to see her first, but they directed me straight to the conference room instead. I got a glance in Jaylee's room, and it was full of doctors and maroon scrubs (surgery team), so I knew things weren't good. A doctor then came in and said, "I need your consent to put Jaylee on ECMO. She became very sick all of a sudden, and we don't have many answers right now, but she needs the ECMO support ASAP." Brandon and I broke down after having sat there for almost an hour with very few updates. My mind began to wander. *Was my baby still alive?* Then her surgeon and another doctor came into the conference room to speak with us. Jaylee was now on ECMO (extracorporeal membrane oxygenation), they told us, and remained stable at that point. They shared with us that the nurse noticed her blood pressure had started dropping, and Jaylee went into cardiac arrest. They did a few compressions until they could get her placed on ECMO, and the rest of the night would be spent figuring out why this happened so suddenly. They were going to make sure it wasn't early signs of rejection, but they needed to keep her stable and let her body and heart rest.

The next day was much better. The tests did not point to any signs of rejection, and all numbers were improving. Even though doctors seemed fairly confident that it wasn't early rejection happening, her team still decided to treat her for rejection to be sure nothing was missed because it was better to be proactive instead of reactive. A few days went by, and the medical team was able to dial back her ECMO support. This meant she wasn't relying on the life support as much. A few more days passed, which allowed her a chance to recover. Jaylee was removed from ECMO support four days later, and her heart was doing 100% of the work and was working beautifully!

After the transplant surgery, Jaylee's chest was not closed. They do this to avoid pressure on the heart and because of all the initial swelling. Closing her chest was now the next big goal. This took a couple of attempts; in fact, three to be exact. Her stats kept dropping with the first couple of attempts, but the third time was a charm! This huge hurdle was now behind us. Jaylee's journey, or should I say *marathon*, included many hurdles of different sizes along the way, but we FINALLY felt like Jaylee was approaching the shorter hurdles. It was an amazing feeling to see her obstacles shrink from mountains, to hills, to eventually speed bumps. The next few goals were to wean her from her oxygen support, taper her pain medication, and get her home. They would need to establish a medication regimen for Jaylee, and they hoped she would tolerate more feeds through her nasogastric (NG) tube. The next week, Jaylee made a lot of progress. She was extubated, her chest tubes were removed, and Brandon and I memorized her home medication regimen. Jaylee was moved to a room closer to the doors, and those rooms were for the less critical patients, so these were all good things!

More great news continued as the days went by. Jaylee was on room air, with no breathing support at all; she was eating and tolerating feeds well; her echo tests looked amazing with good heart function. AND JAYLEE GRADUATED FROM THE PICU! This was a huge accomplishment. Typically, that means home is only a couple of weeks, or even days, away. We could only imagine the thought of leaving and going home with our Jaylee. At times, it scared us, and we definitely had a lot of nerves, but we were so ready. I was in disbelief that the word *home* was now in our conversations.

Home at last! All they had to do was say the word and we were packing up. Of course, things would be different because we were going home to the transplant life of a 10-month-old, but it was still life! These were Jaylee's bonus days that we had dreamed of. All of the love, support, visits, calls, and prayers during this journey helped make it possible for Brandon and me to remain by Jaylee's side during her fight. Her fight was against all odds … but she did it! She proved so many wrong, and she showed the whole world that miracles do happen. There we were, walking out of the place we had called home for a total of 130 days with our miracle. We were on our way home—as a family of three, like it was meant to be.

Today, Jaylee is four years old. Transplant life has been both challenging and amazing. Jaylee has been able to swim, play with friends, see family, go to therapy sessions, attend a day health program, go to the zoo, go camping, and even start preschool. She is also going to be a big sister! All because of organ donation.

About Kelli

Kelli and her husband, Brandon, met in high school, and after getting married five years later, they knew right away that they wanted to start a family someday. Jaylee is their miracle and the reason for everything they do. She has given Kelli a purpose and taught her more about life than anyone ever could have. Jaylee has shown her parents what a true hero is. She is the reason behind Kelli's involvement in organizations such as Help-A-Heart, Tori's Angels, and the Iowa Donor Network.

Kelli and Brandon live in Iowa and are blessed with two amazing daughters, and a huge support system of family and friends.

Feel free to connect with Kelli via social media.

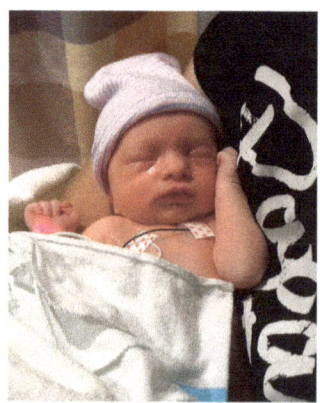

*July 3rd, 2018—We welcomed
Jaylee into our world.*

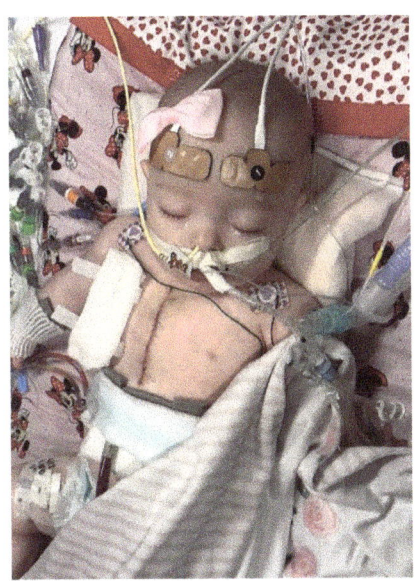

Feb. 2019—After Jaylee's first open heart surgery to place LVAD.

2019—On LVAD waiting for new heart. Our first Jaylee Strong t-shirts!

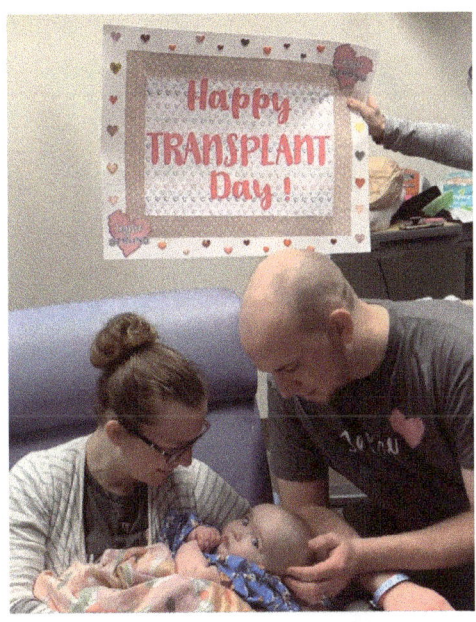

April 26, 2019—Transplant surgery day. Just minutes before Jaylee went to the O.R. for her new heart!

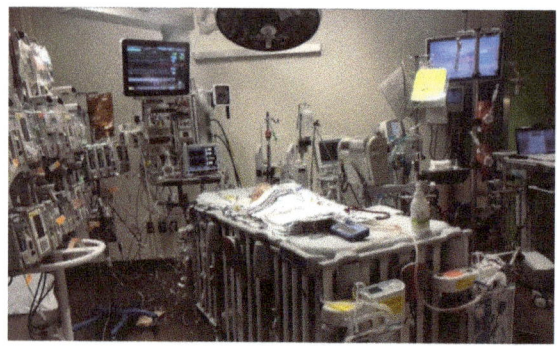

April 27, 2019—Day after transplant surgery.

2019—Home after transplant.

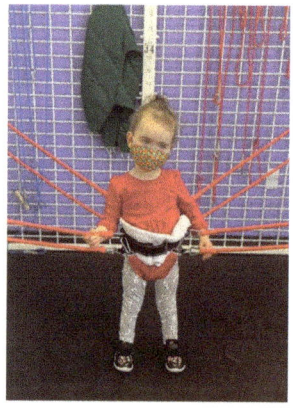

After transplant—working hard at physical therapy.

Celebrating Donate Life month.

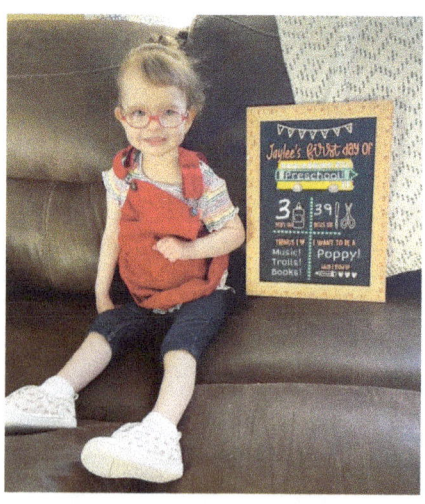

2021—1ˢᵗ day of school!

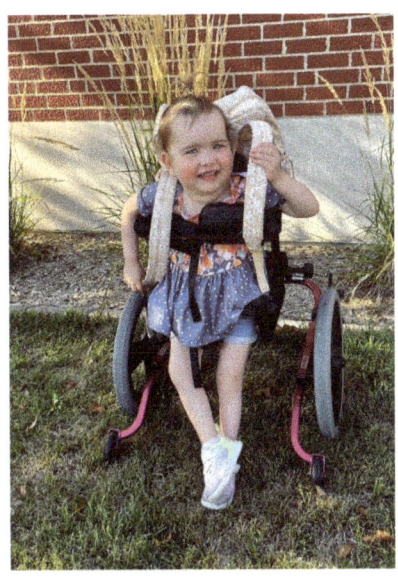

*2022—Ready to start
her second year of school.*

2022—Our family of 4. Jaylee is now a big sister!

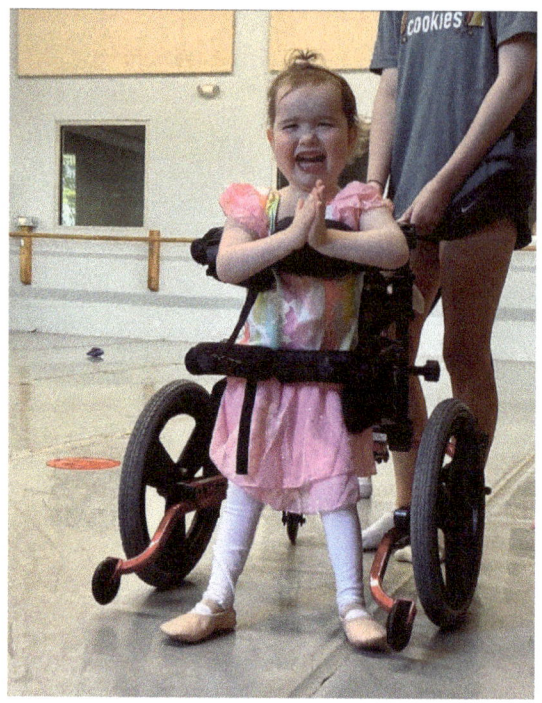

2022—First ever dance class!

2023—Jaylee with her little sister, Reese.

Smilin' Rylen

By Kristen Cowan, with Jamie Porter

While we went through the drawers in his room, I sat holding the clothes he used to wear. I couldn't stop the tears from falling on them. How I wish he were still here.

I see his name on the stool my uncle gave him. Engraved: R-Y-L-E-N. He was supposed to be standing on this, to reach the sink and wash his hands. It sits in the corner. Untouched, collecting dust, about to collect my tears.

I look over on the dresser, and there is a picture of him in my arms at birth. We became a family of four. Complete! But now, it's incomplete. Why is he gone? Tears fall, burning as they stream down my checks.

Let me tell you about our angel, Rylen. Although his life was quick here on Earth, through our loss, he gave gifts… gifts of life.

Where We Lost Our Angel

One Saturday morning, while shopping for jewelry with my twin sister at our local Kendra Scott store for our birthday, I rushed home after receiving a phone call that Rylen was not feeling well; he was fighting a fever. When I walked in the house, I had never seen him look so lifeless and so full of pain. He couldn't tell me how sick he was. I just knew I had to get him to the hospital quickly.

We rushed him to the local hospital, and they ran many tests. The tests resulted in "suspicion" of bacterial meningitis. After a one-night stay at the Memorial Hermann Katy Hospital and determining that Rylen would need more medical procedures, such as a spinal tap, we were transported to the main campus at Children's Memorial Hermann Hospital in downtown Houston. Riding in the ambulance was the longest ride of my life, with all its unknowns and worst-case scenarios playing in my mind. I was grateful, though, for the helpful hands from the paramedics as they quickly assisted Rylen for treatment. It was later confirmed that he had bacterial meningitis. Their suspicions were correct. My heart dropped. What did that mean?

The doctors and nurses quickly worked on him, and I will never forget standing in the corner, crying hysterically and praying to God for a miracle. The doctors were gentle and kind but also frank about the fact that he might not have a lot of time left. With a 25-day regimen of prescription medication for bacterial meningitis, they stated, "Some kids make it, and some do not."

Best Day

After a few hard days in the hospital, and in the midst of the unknown, Rylen showed us a day of hope when he started to display signs of improvement. He tried to open his eyes and let us know that he was grateful for the help we were giving him. We even let his older brother, Corbyn, come up to visit him, and I finally got to hold Rylen after begging the nurses to have him in my arms just one more time. While this was his best day, it was also the beginning of his worst day, as he quickly slipped away…

Worse Days to Follow

…right through our hands. Rylen's health quickly declined. I'll never forget the beeping of the machines, and the doctors rushing into the room to try and figure out what was going on. They had no answers. We had to wait to see if there was life left. One last test was supposed to confirm that. While we waited, LifeGift met with us to ask if we were willing to say "YES" to life, after death, through organ donation.

The test then confirmed there was "no life." In spite of our desperate prayers, in spite of the doctors' fight to keep Rylen alive, God had another plan. We had to let go and let God take it from there.

June 5th, 2017, we lost our angel, Rylen, at 13.5 months old. After a short, nine-day battle with bacterial meningitis, our sweet boy left this earth. Our lives were forever changed. The hidden gift, however, was the gift of saying "YES" to organ donation. Rylen became our hero, and the hero to five other individuals. His short life impacted so many, leaving a ripple effect that still touches the lives of countless people to this day.

Rylen's Heart

First, we had to swallow the fact that God had another plan. God had planned to use Rylen's gifts as a miracle to save others. Even though Rylen had just turned one, he was able to gift his heart to a two-year-old boy. Gannon is now a healthy six-year-old, living and thriving. Back in 2018, my family was able to fly out to Alabama and meet his family. I personally got to listen to Rylen's heart beating in Gannon's chest with an orange stethoscope my friend had given me. My healing began when I heard that beat. That moment is a moment I will never forget: my baby's heart beating inside another boy's chest, giving him life.

I remember holding Gannon at the edge of the lake and having a moment, just the two of us. A lady walked up and asked me if this was my son, and I said, "Well, yes, and no. You see, I lost my son a year ago, and this little boy has his heart beating in his chest. So technically no, he is not my son. But, kind of, because my son's heart is beating inside of him." I call Gannon, "Rylen's heart keeper." To this day, we keep in contact with the family, sending pictures back and forth. We vicariously live through sweet Gannon, as Rylen would be about the same age. We are thankful that the family keeps in contact and that they allow us to connect whenever we need.

Gannon's family had one more act of kindness for us. It is a gift I will never be able to say "Thank you" enough for. Shortly before Gannon turned six, he was adopted by his great aunt. When she adopted him, she explained that he would have a new last name. She also mentioned that he could change his middle name. I immediately mentioned that Rylen's middle name was Quinn and jokingly suggested they could change it to that. To my surprise, when he was officially adopted, he took on Rylen's middle name. I am happy to report that Gannon's new name is now Gannon Quinn! What a beautiful tribute to our Rylen… Gannon's hero.

Rylen's Liver

The discovery of Rylen's liver transplant story was a bit unorthodox. It all started with a Facebook post from a friend of mine, asking for prayers for their friend, whose two-year-old daughter, Cameron, was getting a new liver. This all was around the same time that Rylen's organs were being matched. With goosebumps all over, I immediately knew, as a mother's heart just knows, that this sweet little girl had to be the one who was receiving Rylen's liver. After my friend connected us through Facebook, we continued messaging back and forth, matching the dates when Cameron received her liver and when Rylen gave his organs. The final confirmation came when Cameron's family asked their Organ Procurement Organization (OPO) to confirm if there was a note from the donor family. The OPO pulled out a letter that I had written. This solidified all our suspicions, confirming that Rylen was indeed Cameron's liver donor.

When dates were set to meet the family, Cameron was not feeling well, so we decided to skip our meeting. We wanted to respect Cameron and her health and only meet her and her family when she was at her best. Unfortunately, we never had the opportunity to meet Cameron and her family, as this was when her body went into rejection.

Cameron only had Rylen's gift for a little more than a year. I was devastated to hear this news, as Rylen's gift was no longer serving its purpose for Cameron. I had to retrain my brain to remember an important fact about organ donation. When people receive their transplanted organ, it always acts as a second chance at life, but sometimes, the time frame may be shorter for some than for others. At the end of the day, when a recipient receives their transplanted organ, it ultimately is a beautiful gift. Even though the purpose of Rylen's liver for Cameron was for a shorter amount of time, nonetheless, it was still a gift. Any amount of time is a gift worth giving, or a gift worth receiving… the ultimate gift of life.

My "momma heart" is at peace, knowing that Cameron, who is now six, is doing well. She is living her best life with another liver given to her as a special gift, just like Rylen's was. I appreciate Cameron's family allowing me to check in every so often to see how she is doing, and to see her continue to grow and remain healthy. The best part is, even though Cameron no longer has Rylen's liver, they are forever grateful for the gift of time that was given to their daughter, and they don't take any of that time for granted.

Rylen's Intestine and Right Kidney

With a heavy heart, I must write that I am not in contact with the recipients of Rylen's intestine and right kidney. For many reasons unknown to me, they did not respond or reply back to the letters that I wrote. I do know that one recipient was an 11-year-old boy; he received Rylen's intestine. The other recipient was the oldest of all the recipients; a 49-year-old male received Rylen's right kidney. Though we are not in communication, I have found peace, imagining that Rylen's recipients are happy and healthy, and living their best life, thankful for Rylen's gift. Whether I ever hear back from them or not, I will continue to think of them daily and pray continuously for their health.

Rylen's Left Kidney

If you have counted correctly, you will realize I still have one more donor recipient to introduce you to. The last one I want to tell you about is a sweet and kind gentleman, now 46-years-old, named Brian. Brian is Rylen's left kidney recipient, and he lives close enough that we have visited with him and his family three times. I find so much joy in Brian for many reasons. First, it always shocks people to hear that a 41-year-old man received a 13.5-month-old's left kidney. It was a very successful match! Brian often stays in contact and shares words of gratitude that the other recipients can't share (due to age or disconnect). Brian calls Rylen his "hero" and his "wingman." He is able to speak of the gravity of his gift. Brian shared with us a time when he was really sick and almost did not make it. His body was rejecting his first organ transplant, but then he got the call for his new kidney. He had a successful transplant surgery and recovery, and now he can live his life with fulfillment and not in fear. Brian is thriving and gives thought to Rylen each day, living his life with its endless possibilities. Our relationship is very close, and I cherish it deeply. All I have to do is message him, or call him, and I can feel just a little bit closer to Rylen. When we said "YES" to organ donation, our family grew! Thank you to Brian for being a part of our family! Because of organ donation, Rylen lives on in others, through others.

Kendra Scott Catches Our Grief

Flashback to the Kendra Scott birthday shopping event where it all began. The day after that trip, my sister Jamie received a short email survey asking about her experience. Such a dichotomous moment of joy for a beautiful birthday jewelry gift, and yet an overwhelming sadness for the beginning journey of an ultimate loss. When Kendra Scott received my sister's survey response explaining the events of her tragic day, they knew they had to meet us. They wanted to hear Rylen's story and help find a way to support us in our grief. A Kendra Scott jewelry store nearby asked us to be part of a community fundraising event called "Kendra Gives Back" where 20% of the sales on a certain day would go to an organization of our choice. We are forever grateful for how Kendra Scott turned our tears of sorrow into tears of joy for "giving back," quite parallel to organ donation and the gift of life. With the success of our first fundraising event, we were able to raise $3,500, which we chose to give directly to LifeGift.

LifeGift Transport Car

While deciding what to do with the funds donated to LifeGift, my family arrived at the idea of doing a car wrap with Rylen's precious face on it. I thought this was the perfect project to spend the donated money on, as it would serve as a reminder and encourage everyone to become an organ donor. We wanted a young baby's face to show that even a 13.5-month-old could donate organs and save lives. Age is not a factor! You too can be a hero like Rylen.

Within a few months, in the summer of 2018, the car wrap was complete. To this day, LifeGift's car drives around town, transporting nurses, doctors, and even organs back and forth between LifeGift's headquarters and the main hospitals in the Houston Medical Center, advertising and promoting organ donation.

We feel blessed with this partnership and the support we receive from our local OPO, knowing that Rylen is their spokesperson, traveling around town, encouraging others to say "YES" to organ donation. So proud too, might I add!

Rylen in the Rose Parade

Due to our special relationship with LifeGift, my family was nominated by multiple staff members to travel to Pasadena, California in December of 2019 for the Rose Parade. Rylen's face was chosen to be made into a floragraph to be displayed on the Donate Life Float to debut on New Year's Day, January 1st, 2020! My husband and I were honored to watch the beautiful process: all the precision, detail, dedication, and time that went into creating the rose float where Rylen, along with many other organ donors, would be recognized for all their gifts. We are thankful for this once-in-a-lifetime opportunity and for the memories stored in our hearts because of this event. We will forever cherish this experience as we pass Rylen's floragraph, proudly hung in the hallway of our home, gifted by LifeGift.

With the closing of the Rose Parade, and the trip of a lifetime, we knew we had to do more to keep Rylen's memory alive. We were just getting started with God's plan, as we knew we wanted to keep spreading awareness about organ donation. This determination and drive are what fueled the beginning of our next chapter, the birth of the "Smilin' Rylen Foundation."

Race for Rylen

When Rylen earned his angel wings, I knew in my heart that I wanted to honor him by starting a foundation to help keep his memory alive, but also to help families going through a tragedy like ours. I most definitely wanted a platform that everyone could relate to, which is why the foundation's mission is to help families in crisis and to raise awareness about organ donation.

When we went through the steps to establish ourselves as a non-profit organization, we had to come up with a name. I knew immediately that I wanted to call it "The Smilin' Rylen Foundation." Rylen had the nickname "Smilin' Rylen" because he was always SMILING! I knew that by naming the foundation after him, we could make sure that others continued SMILIN', just like our Smilin' Rylen. On August 18th, 2017, only two months after Rylen earned his angel wings, "The Smilin' Rylen Foundation" was born, along with the idea to host an annual run.

In April of 2018 (only ten months after we lost Rylen), we hosted our very first "Smilin' Rylen Run" in Rylen's honor. We pick the month of April annually, because it is Rylen's birthday month (April 11th). Coincidentally, we discovered that April is also Donate Life Month, and conveniently, the last week of April leading up to the race is National Pediatric Transplant Week. I'm pretty sure that Rylen had his little hand in all of this, making sure these dates fit perfectly for April, to simultaneously align with the foundation's mission.

What can you expect to see on the day of our annual race? You'll see a community of sponsors, families, friends, children, dogs, beneficiaries, and LOVE. You'll see runners, walkers, donated food, laughter, face painting, balloon artists, and even the LifeGift car with Rylen's face on the side. But most importantly, you will see the overwhelming support pouring out to surround my family as we celebrate Rylen's life and his gifts given, and you will FEEL Rylen smilin' down, beaming from ear to ear, within your heart.

We couldn't be more proud of what has been accomplished through "The Smilin' Rylen Foundation" and annual runs. We know that Rylen is PROUD of us too! All the love, support, and prayers amassed over the past five years has helped us raise more than $200,000, which has gone directly to our beautiful beneficiaries.

Our Beneficiaries

Let me introduce you to our beneficiaries. Each of these organizations were handpicked and chosen, as they directly supported my family throughout our darkest days and the most challenging parts of losing Rylen. We wanted to be able to give back in our grieving and healing process to help other families who might be going through something similar. Through this act of giving back, my family truly has had the opportunity to turn our heartbreak into joy, knowing that others are benefiting from the funds of the Smilin' Rylen Run.

LifeGift

Our first beneficiary is LifeGift, which is the OPO that supported our family by matching Rylen's gifts, so carefully gifting them to five other individuals ranging from 2 to 49 years of age. Anyone can become an organ donor, despite race, gender, or religion. You too can be a hero like Rylen because of organ donation. To learn more about LifeGift, organ donation, and the opportunity to become an organ donor, you can visit their website at www.lifegift.org.

Ronald McDonald House Houston

The second beneficiary we give to is the Ronald McDonald House in Houston, which houses families who have a loved one being taken care of in the medical center long term. Though my family was only in the hospital nine days total from beginning to end, the wing of the hospital we stayed in, at Children's Memorial Hermann Hospital, had rooms available with a bed, chair, TV, bathroom, and a common kitchen for gathering, cooking, and eating. I cannot even begin to explain the comfort this brought to my family. It meant so much to have the ability to stay each night down the hall from Rylen. This allowed us to have a place to lay our sleepy heads, a place to wash up, and a place to gather and eat. "A home away from home" is what was provided for my family, taking away the burden of driving back and forth to our home in Katy, or having to spend money on a hotel. For long-term housing in the medical center, check out the Ronald McDonald House Houston at www.rmhhouston.org.

Emma's Hugs

Our third beneficiary is a smaller organization called Emma's Hugs. Emma's Hugs provides parking assistance to families in the Houston Medical Center. Thanks to Emma's Hugs, we had parking coverage the entire time we were there and were relieved of the financial burden that goes with daily parking, which is about $18 a day. Emma's Hugs provides a gift that any family staying long term in the hospital would truly benefit from. We are happy to share and spread word about this wonderful organization. Check out their website if you would like to refer someone to receive a parking pass in the form of an Emma's "hug" at www.emmashugs.org.

Now I Lay Me Down to Sleep

Our fourth beneficiary is an organization called Now I Lay Me Down to Sleep. This organization was established to provide remembrance photography for families during those last moments in the hospital. My family received a beautiful keepsake photo album that we visit each year, and we are thankful for the memories it holds. Pictures are truly worth a million words. We are blessed with the opportunity to share and support this amazing organization and to help promote their mission: providing the gift of remembrance portraits to parents experiencing the death of a baby. To learn more about their non-profit, visit their website at www.nowilaymedowtosleep.org.

Bo's Place

In addition to our four beneficiaries, we also give back to Bo's Place with money raised specifically from our annual online raffle, which is part of the Smilin' Rylen Run. Bo's Place exists to provide grief group support to those who have experienced loss. Bo's Place has provided wonderful support to my family over the last five years. Grief is hard and can feel lonely. Knowing that you are not alone on this grief journey, that you are alongside others, can be very comforting. Being able to share the feelings you experience while grieving and being given the tools to help you navigate unexpected loss is healing. There are groups for the entire family, including kids, which was a bonus for us, as we were needing something for Rylen's older brother, Corbyn. If you have experienced any loss, at any level, Bo's Place might be the right place for you and your family. Visit their website at www.bosplace.org.

Life After Loss: Rylen's Legacy

I would have never believed you if you told me that I would be the founder of a non-profit organization, that Rylen would inspire people to become organ donors, that a beautiful annual run would raise over $200,000 for giving back to families in need, and that I'd experience personal healing with every gift given. Never in my wildest dreams would I believe that our most tragic moment would transform me and my family into the creation of a LEGACY... of RYLEN'S LEGACY. Every day, I am proud that I didn't give up hope, and that I didn't give into the idea of just sitting in a corner and crying myself into misery, as a person might do after experiencing the tragic and unimaginable loss of a child. I am thankful God had a plan, a plan I could not see, a plan I just had to TRUST IN, that only HE could orchestrate... of course, with help from Rylen.

Our Promise to Rylen

We promise to never forget you, Rylen, by doing all that we can to help as many families as possible and to continue raising awareness about organ donation. We promise to remember you when we see your favorite color, orange, in the beautiful sunrises and sunsets, along with every orange butterfly that flies across our path. On our sad days, we will look for "Rylen winks," which are orange signs sent to us from you. We promise we will continue to perform acts of kindness in your memory, and to never stop saying your name: Rylen.

Our Love Letter to Rylen

Dear Rylen,

Your dad, brother, and I will forever hold you in our hearts. We know you are forever SMILIN' down on us from Heaven. One day soon, we will reunite forever, but until then, we will continue to make you proud as you have made us proud. We love you Rylen, Smilin' Rylen. Forever in our hearts.

Mommy, Daddy, and Corbyn

About Kristen

Kristen Cowan is married to Travis Cowan, and they live in Katy, Texas. Their son, Corbyn, is nine and "Angel" Rylen would be six. Kristen, bravely in her grief, grew The Smilin Rylen Foundation (SRF) to advocate for organ donation, to support families in crisis, and most importantly, to keep Rylen's smile remembered! 2023 is her sixth year putting on the race in his memory! She diligently pushes through to advocate for her beneficiaries, to love on other "Angel" moms, and to continue healing in her grief as she keeps Rylen's name alive.

About Jamie

Jamie Porter is the identical twin sister to Kristen Cowan, and co-writer on this chapter. She resides in Pearland, Texas and is married to Brian Porter. They have two boys Zack (10) and Alex (8). The boys miss and love their "Angel" cousin, Rylen, just as much as their Aunt Jamie does. Jamie is the number-one supporter of anything Rylen, from grief support, gather support, to SRF support, and she is lucky to be a 2023 sponsor of the SRF race! By training, Jamie is a family therapist, which allows her to understand the deeper needs of grief and its effects on the body. Jamie loves advocating for grief support, organ donation, and reminding people who Rylen was.

Never forgotten! Always in our hearts!

Rylen's favorite place to be!

My family of 4…. forever!

Me meeting Gannon for the first time in 2018, and listening to Rylen's heart beating inside Gannon's chest.

Gannon and I, meeting up in Alabama, the moment I had been waiting for!

The "LifeGift" car with the Rylen car wrap, advocating organ donation, driving around the Houston medical center!

Our favorite picture of Smilin' Rylen! Can you see why that was his nickname?

This time, Brian came to visit us in Katy, Texas to meet my family!

Brian Green and I meeting for the first time in Roanoke, Texas, in 2019. He is the left kidney recipient. (46 years of age now)

Rylen's beautiful Floragraph placed on Donate Life's Rose Parade Float New Year's Day 2020!

This is our Smilin' Rylen Foundation logo! Orange for Rylen's favorite color, green for organ donation, and the foundation words in a "smile" format!

Smilin' Rylen Race Day! (Year 4-2021)
planning for Smilin' Rylen Run year 6-2023.

Travis and I at the 5th annual Smilin'
Rylen Run! Yard sign donated to our event!

My twin sister, Jamie, is my best friend and has been by my side through everything. All the ups and downs of life, and I'm just so thankful she helped me co-write, as I couldn't have done it with out her!

This is our registration flyer for our race this year, April 29th, 2023! QR code takes you straight to our website where everything is housed from Rylen's story, who we give back to, a live donate button, and registration for our annual race!

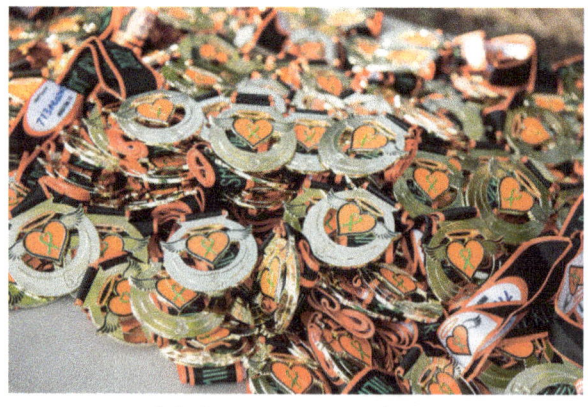

Race medals from year 5! Each participant gets a medal when they cross the finish line!

Smiles For Phia

By Stephanie Skrede, with Kayla Fink

The things we learn to anticipate
Often come with joy and strife
Which one is never known
But both can change a life

It was a cold November morning, just a few days after my sixteenth birthday. The winter chill in the air brought with it a blanket of anticipation, an anticipation that had been accumulating for weeks. It was hard to believe the day had finally arrived. It was the day I would take my driver's test. As I prepared to walk out the front door, I envisioned all the opportunities that would accompany the privilege to drive a car. I could hardly contain my excitement! The event itself was a blur, from passing the written exam, to meeting all the requirements of the road test. I barely noticed the camera flash when it came time to take the headshot for my license photo. But passing the exams and being granted the ability to drive on my own wasn't the milestone I attributed to this day. The milestone was placing the orange organ donor sticker on my license. Little did I know the impact organ donation would have on my future family, but I proudly placed my sticker and was prepared to save a life, or lives, through organ donation if the time came.

Sixteen years later, my husband Arvid and I were expecting our fourth child: a daughter we named Sophia. Sophia was the perfect addition to our family. She was tiny and had the cutest squeaky cry. We were all in love. After her birth, as the weeks passed, something seemed off. She would eat constantly but was unable to hold anything down. Her growth was slow, and the typical breastfeeding jaundice wasn't fading. Her stools weren't the normal color. We were reassured she was doing fine, but in the back of our minds, something felt off. No one else noticed or commented until a family outing prompted a close friend to ask if Sophia was okay. The friend worked in a daycare, in close proximity to babies. Her concern made us realize that our own concerns needed further investigation, so we immediately sought additional medical direction.

We made an appointment for Sophia to be re-evaluated and have a panel of blood work done. The results came back quickly and revealed a need for further testing. The second round of testing prompted a referral to a pediatric gastroenterologist. That appointment happened to fall on our ten-year wedding anniversary. Arvid was confident the appointment would end with a simple prescription, but I feared the worst.

The day of Sophia's gastroenterologist appointment came quickly and was met with a dark sense of anticipation. Unlike the anticipation I felt the day I took my driver's test, this felt heavy. Instead of anticipating new opportunities, I would be learning to expect uncertainty. As we sat in the room, barely breathing, the doctor entered. She was very straightforward in her stature and nature, and she asked if we were familiar with biliary atresia. We weren't, but we could tell that the explanation to follow would not be accompanied by good news. She proceeded to explain that biliary atresia was a rare pediatric liver disease with no known cause and no known cure, and she suspected specialized testing would confirm this as Sophia's diagnosis. The only treatment was a surgical procedure called a *Kasai*. If that procedure failed, the only chance of survival would be through a liver transplant. The odds of a successful Kasai procedure were slim, since Sophia was already over three months old. Our hearts sank, and the earlier sense of anticipation immediately turned to dread and fear – not of the unknown, but of the reality that was about to become ours.

After being allowed just a few moments to digest the news of Sophia's suspected diagnosis, we were rushed to the nearest children's hospital to obtain final confirmation. Nothing could prepare us for what we were about to witness Sophia go through. The testing was rigorous, and our sense of helplessness only intensified after seeing each test performed. The tests confirmed that Sophia did indeed have biliary atresia, a rare disease that affects only one in 15,000 live births a year. Sophia's Kasai procedure was scheduled for just three days later.

The Kasai procedure went well, and after less than a week of inpatient care, we were discharged with over fifteen medications, and a lot of hope and fear. Being home as a family felt amazing, but that feeling quickly changed when Sophia developed a fever and abdominal distention. Tests in our local ER revealed that the surgical connections had come loose and that emergency surgery was needed. We followed the ambulance to the children's hospital, and the cycle of anticipation started all over again, as it became clear a liver transplant would be our only hope.

In the coming days, our medical team prepared us for all scenarios and obstacles. Sophia was very tiny, and the chances of finding a donor liver that her body could accommodate would be difficult. The option of pursuing a living donor was brought up, but the odds were equally daunting. With Sophia being so tiny, we would have to find an adult just the right size to be a match. We left for home feeling defeated. We questioned everything, and most of all, we questioned our strength and ability to face it.

The coming weeks included regular appointments, labs, and tests. We watched as Sophia gradually became weaker and more yellow.

We did absolutely everything in our power to keep life as "normal" as possible for her and our older children. If Sophia didn't survive, we didn't want to waste the days she lived. We wanted her to experience life. Sophia did just that as she played and reached milestones like our big kids, but at a slower pace due to her distended abdomen and weakness from a failing liver. She powered through medications and smiled at every turn. Our amazing daughter was the hope we needed to face whatever the future had in store. Her love and zest for life helped suppress the heavy anticipation that lurked in the corner of every room we walked into.

By the end of summer 2013, it was time to begin yet another chapter of our journey, which was the transplant workup. This new chapter also brought with it a change in treatment facilities. The new facility showed us how to best care for Sophia and how to keep her as comfortable as possible. Within just days of being listed for a transplant, Sophia was approved for a living donor.

Upon approval for a living donor, we were quickly instructed on the process for locating a suitable match. We started with ourselves. Unfortunately, I am the wrong blood type, but Arvid was a match. We were also asked to submit packets for anyone else wanting to be tested. It was completely anonymous, and we would only be notified if a match was found and the applicant was willing to proceed. I quickly updated my social media in a desperate plea for help. In response to my plea, I received a text from our friend Kayla. She was the one who encouraged us to have Sophia's condition re-evaluated. Kayla indicated that she had the right blood type and wanted to try to save Sophia. She submitted a testing packet, along with thirteen other individuals. With each new packet submitted, and with Arvid as a potential match, we felt a step closer to hope.

After what felt like months, we received a call notifying us that Arvid was simply too tall for his liver to match Sophia's size, but there was a potential donor that appeared perfect… on paper anyway. We were informed that this person would be notified, and further testing would begin.

The wait and uncertainty were agonizing. We had no idea who had been sent for additional testing, or if they would end up being a viable match for Sophia. Once again, anticipation set in, but this time around what might *not* happen. Then, one phone call from a friend changed everything. Kayla called to tell us that she was Sophia's match on paper, and she was the one undergoing the additional testing.

Kayla is kind-hearted and funny, and she is equipped with a smile that can turn even the heaviest frown upside down. We had always seen Kayla as a source of joy in our lives, but never thought she would be the one to save us... to save our daughter's life.

A friend is one who anticipates
That you'll need guidance through the strife
But Kayla is more than just a friend
She's the angel that saved our life

Kayla was sent for further testing and informed that she would be notified in a few weeks of her status as a match for Sophia. The waiting and the not knowing was almost unbearable. I couldn't focus on anything except the phone ringing. In the meantime, Sophia's yellow coloration continued to deepen. She vomited often and lost a great deal of weight. You could touch her stomach and physically feel her ailing liver. Family and friends struggled to hold her for fear of hurting her. A feeding tube was ultimately placed to aid in Sophia's growth and nourishment. Through all the trials and tribulations, Sophia continued to face the world with a smile. Her energy and positivity were the driving forces behind our ability to remain optimistic.

On a Friday evening, several weeks after Kayla's testing, we settled in for a quiet night at home. Our big kids were asleep, and Sophia was hooked up to her nightly feeds. It was, all things considered, a normal night within the scope of our "new normal." But an unexpected knock at the door would again change everything in an instant. Kayla and a mutual friend were standing on the other side of our door with a gift bag in hand. I wasn't sure what to expect upon greeting their unexpected presence, but before I knew it, I was holding the content of the gift bag: a tiny shirt that read "Keep Calm, We're a match." Kayla unzipped her jacket to reveal her own matching shirt, and I immediately burst into tears. The gift bag contained the greatest gift we had ever been given: a chance at life for our precious Sophia. A sense of hope filled our family.

Once the news of Kayla's status as a match was revealed, we were briefed by Sophia's medical team. They indicated that they would only use Kayla as a living liver donor if a deceased donor wasn't found in time. They would wait as long as possible, knowing they had Kayla as a match if necessary. Just before Christmas, 2013, when Sophia was just nine months old, it was time to move forward. She was starting to bleed, was not gaining weight, and was getting weaker by the day. Surgery was scheduled for the end of December, so we made Christmas memories with our kids and then packed it away quickly to focus on the journey ahead.

The days following Christmas were difficult. What is typically a joyous time of year was wrought with medical complications and general discomfort for Sophia. The decision was made to admit her a day early to prevent further struggling prior to transplant. The night before her surgery was met with a flurry of anticipation. We anticipated the relief that would come with a successful surgery, and the opportunity that would come with her improved health. There was also the fear and heartache that would come with waiting for the results of the surgery itself. I spent the entire night holding Sophia in a rocking chair, studying every detail of her sweet self and working through every layer of anticipation I felt. I could not fathom putting her down for even a moment.

Morning came before I could even begin to feel ready. We gave Sophia hugs and kisses and sent her off to the OR. I could not stand the thought of waiting through the estimated eight to fifteen-hour surgery. I was consumed with worry, not only for Sophia, but for Kayla as well. Kayla had become family to us, and having two family members in the operating room simultaneously was almost more than I could manage.

During Sophia's surgery, the minutes passed as if they were hours. I couldn't focus and stayed glued to the phone for an update. There was always the possibility that when Kayla's liver was assessed in real time, it wouldn't be a viable match after all. The prospect of getting this far in the process only to have our hopes shattered consumed my thoughts.

Finally, a phone call came in letting us know that part of Kayla's liver was on its way to Sophia. Soon after, another call informed us that blood was flowing to Sophia's new liver. Each call set off a new wave of emotion. Just as we thought we had cried all the tears we had, the thought of seeing Sophia and Kayla after a successful surgery re-opened the floodgates. Kayla was soon moved out of the operating room and into her own room. Seeing her for the first time after surgery was like seeing Sophia right after she was born. My heart was bursting with love and gratitude.

After thirteen hours, Sophia's surgery was finally complete. The anticipation of seeing her was intertwined with the fear of the unknown. We had no idea what to expect. It was a shock, at first, to see the myriad of machines and medical staff surrounding her tiny body, but there was already a noticeable difference in her health. The yellowness of her skin had faded, and she looked healthier than she had in many months. Our hopes and dreams for Sophia's future all congregated in her hospital room, and at that very moment, we knew they would all come true. While we spent New Year's Eve in the hospital, we felt a renewed sense of hope. Seeing the positive changes in Sophia's health was overwhelming. Faith, hope, and love had always been our foundation, and this moment was no different.

In the coming days, we quickly experienced the rollercoaster of post-transplant life. Kayla was released to a local hotel soon after her surgery and was allowed to return home after one week. The same day Kayla was sent home, Sophia was taken back for a clean-up and assessment. Just days later, her breathing tube was removed, and we heard Sophia's sweet little voice for the first time in over a week. Tears rolled down the faces of everyone present, and once again, we knew that our dreams for Sophia's future would become reality.

The weeks following Sophia's surgery brought progress. Her condition continued to improve, and two weeks after surgery, she was discharged to the Ronald McDonald House. Our older children joined us, and after nearly a month-long separation, we were finally all together as a family. Five weeks later, we were released to go home. We returned weekly for check-ups, as we adjusted to our new normal. Arvid and I continued to count our blessings for Sophia's second chance at life.

Sophia is now an active ten-year-old who absolutely loves life and enjoys every moment. She has progressed from taking over eighteen medications, multiple times a day, to taking one anti-rejection medication once a day. Sophia makes it her priority to live life to the fullest. She takes care of her liver by eating healthy and getting in lots of activities. Our girl doesn't take a second for granted. Sophia has always been a light. She has persevered through life's challenges and shown strength, even as an infant, and more so now. We continue to have twice yearly appointments with her medical team and labs every three months. We not only celebrate Sophia's birthday, but also her "liver-versary" with Kayla to mark the life-changing milestone. Kayla has become a part of our immediate family, and she is a regular at family events and family portrait sessions.

We have made it our mission to not only advocate for Sophia and her medical needs, but to raise awareness for organ donation, blood donation, and biliary atresia to help others experiencing medical hardship. Our hope is to provide opportunities for continued medical advancements that will award other families a second chance at life for their children. When I placed that orange organ donation sticker on my license all those years ago, I knew it could be life changing. What I could never anticipate was the impact that organ donation would have on my own life.

Anticipation is part of life

And brings us hope and fear

But looking back, I wouldn't change a thing

Because it kept Sophia here

Kayla's Story

At the time, I had no idea that 2013 would be one of the hardest years of my life – and beyond rewarding at the same time. My mom passed away from terminal brain cancer on March 2nd, 2013. Eleven days later, Sophia Skrede was born. Following my mom's passing, I had taken time away from social media and had decided to get back on nearing my 22nd birthday. Not long after my return, I saw pictures of Sophia that her mom Stephanie had been posting on Facebook. Sophia was a petite, olive-skinned baby whose smile stole the room. Not right away, but soon after those first photos, I noticed that Sophia was different from her siblings. She didn't share their fair skin tone. A mutual friend and I were out to brunch, and I brought up Sophia's skin. I was reassured she was perfectly healthy and had her grandparents' skin.

In early June, I saw Sophia in person for the first time, and I couldn't bite my tongue. I told Stephanie that I thought Sophia's skin was more yellow than olive, and it was more noticeable now in person. My job at the time was caring for infants six weeks to twelve months. Since I had cuddled so many babies, of all different skin tones, something loud inside of me said something was wrong. About a week later, I heard of biliary atresia for the first time, and for some reason, I felt guilty. That quickly changed.

Having just been on a medical journey with my mom, I knew it was hard to ask people for help. I also knew, if the Skrede family needed anything, I was available. Around this time, the bond between Stephanie and I first strengthened. It's really easy to retreat into yourself during difficult times, so I wanted to be there for them because this wasn't going to be an easy road.

When the news came that Sophia would need a new liver, I realized I could help more than I ever expected. A change of hospitals meant Sophia was listed for transplant and the option for a living donor had also opened up. As soon as we knew Sophia and I had the same blood type, I never questioned donating. I had already lived twenty-two years, and by donating part of my liver (which I knew would grow back), Sophia would get the opportunity to live a full life. This was the easiest "yes" of my life. I filled out the paperwork and sent it off. Then we waited.

I received a call from Northwestern to do further testing. At this time, things were not a guarantee, but I had a good feeling. I had another decision to make, which was whether or not to tell the Skrede's that I was testing to be Sophia's living liver donor. If everything moved forward, I had the option to donate anonymously or tell them. I decided to let the Skredes know when the testing would take place, and to please keep it between us until we got the green light.

I went down to Chicago the night before test day so I would be rested beforehand. In the morning, I walked over to Northwestern, and the day began with labs, followed by a presentation with the lead nurse of the transplant program. She went over not only what the testing day would include, but also what the transplant would include and what recovery would be like. After the presentation, we had meetings with the lead nurse, transplant surgeon, and a psychologist. This was an in-depth meeting about the transplant and a time for them to answer any of my questions.

The psychologist was there to make sure it was my decision to donate. They needed to know that I was comfortable with having a scar from surgery and to make sure I understood and was okay with the risks. Not once did I worry about the risks of the surgery. Yes, I knew they existed, but choosing to drive to Chicago for the day of testing carried its own risks. Most of our life decisions carry more risk than choosing to have this surgery. I wasn't worried about the risks or about having a scar. The final step that day was an MRI so the surgeons could examine my liver and compare it to Sophia's. After the MRI, I returned home, and another wait began.

As we waited, I knew how I wanted to tell Stephanie and Arvid if Sophia and I were a match, but I didn't want to jinx things by buying what I'd need until I received the call. On a Friday afternoon in November, the call finally came that we were a match. This meant that if a deceased donor didn't become available, they would proceed with the living donor transplant. After work, I went to the craft store to buy the supplies to make the gift for the Skredes. I had decided to make two custom T-shirts with iron-on letters. Upon finishing the shirts, I drove over to their house. I knocked on the door and handed Stephanie a little pink shirt that read "Keep Calm, We're a Match." There were tears, smiles, laughs, photos, phone calls, and most importantly, a reignited sense of hope. Once more, the wait continued.

While we waited, there were many visits to the Skrede's and a few appointments leading up to the transplant. Then the call came, and a date was set. The night before the transplant, I got to visit Sophia at

Lurie Children's Hospital. I knew everything would be different the next day. Early on December 30th, 2013, I went into Northwestern for the beginning of what would be a long, but very important, day. During pre-op, there was a lot of texting to calm nerves and offer well wishes. A couple of hours later, I was taken back for surgery, then wheeled into recovery with a slightly smaller liver.

Four days after the transplant, I saw Sophia for the first time in person. Even though she was still sedated, I couldn't get over how much better she looked. A few days later, I went home, and my recovery was in full swing. I was off of work for seven weeks with two follow-up appointments in Chicago. When Sophia was released to the Ronald McDonald House, next to Lurie's, I got to see her. She was bubbly and all smiles, spending time with her family, and that was reason enough to be a living donor. I had no regrets.

Within three months, my liver was fully regenerated, and essentially everything for me was back to normal. For the next two years, I had appointments to make sure everything was going according to plan. Today, the only trace of the liver donation is the scar and my connection to Sophia and her family. The transplant not only saved Sophia and gave her time to enjoy her life, but it also brought me a second family and a friendship with Stephanie that is unmatched. Sophia is a light in my life and every life she touches. I had a small role in why she is here, but that little girl has an insurmountable amount of strength, and if you ask me, she gets that from her mom, Stephanie.

One of the best things to come from this journey is also the hardest to put into words. Sophia and I have a connection, and I mean beyond her having my liver inside her. It's a connection that most would never put together and quite unique. Sophia and I see each other now at least once a month, but in the beginning, it was much more frequently. Thankfully, we only live a few miles apart, so it has allowed us to create and nurture a very strong bond. Over time, as Sophia grew into herself, we began to notice she had some of my personality traits and likes/dislikes. For instance, I do a thing that I like to call "an inappropriate whisper" – I whisper in a place where you can just talk normally. Sophia did this, and it stopped Stephanie and Arvid in their tracks. I was nowhere around. For a time, Sophia wouldn't eat apples or carrots either, both of which I am allergic to.

Now, years later, we say "It's the liver," because it's the Kayla in Sophia rather than everyday Sophia. When we first noticed this, Stephanie brought it up to the liver team, and they were very skeptical. We knew what we had seen, however, so it stayed in our minds and our opinion on it didn't change. In time, the liver team started to hear more stories of this happening, and there have been actual studies about it at other transplant centers. They have found that most recipients don't notice these changes, or the new characteristics, because they either received their organ from a deceased donor, or they don't have a close connection to their living donor. In our case, Sophia and I were close from very early on, even before she understood everything about the transplant. The bond is impossible to put into words, and I'm okay with that. It is the part I would never change.

If I had the opportunity to donate again, I would do it in a heartbeat. As I said, this was the easiest decision I've ever made. Becoming a living donor will always be a special experience for me. It is nearly impossible to put into words, but if you are thinking about doing it, I say go for it.

About Stephanie

Stephanie was born and raised in Kaukauna, Wisconsin. She's a licensed cosmetologist but happily a stay-at-home mom. Stephanie married Arvid in June of 2003, and together, they have four kids: Alexis, Spencer, Alizabeth, and Sophia. Sophia was diagnosed with biliary atresia on Stephanie and Arvid's ten-year wedding anniversary. Together, Arvid and Stephanie have made it their mission to advocate for biliary atresia, organ donation, and blood donation. Both Stephanie and Arvid are board members of BARE, Inc., a foundation dedicated to the research and education of biliary atresia.

You can connect with Stephanie on Facebook and Instagram through the "Smiles for Phia" pages.

About Kayla

Kayla was born and raised in Kimberly, Wisconsin by her parents. Stan and Ellen. She has an older brother, Nate, an older half-brother, Heath, and older half-sister, Heather. She has a Labradinger dog named Nellie. Growing up, Kayla lived an active life playing many sports and dancing.

Kayla has worked in the child care industry, and now works as an e-commerce manager. She really enjoys going to work every day, and that is important to her. Kayla enjoys binge watching tv shows, reading, resin crafts, and quilting. She also loves watching and attending NWSL, USWNT, and WNBA games.

Donating part of her liver to Sophia was the easiest *Yes!* she has ever made. If you have questions regarding living liver donation, you can connect with Kayla through the "Smiles for Phia" pages on Facebook and Instagram.

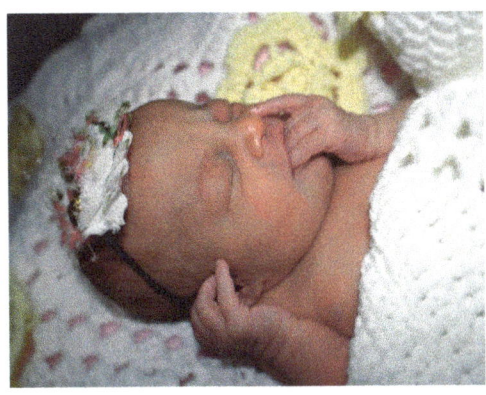

Sophia, days old. Before we knew what the road ahead looked like.

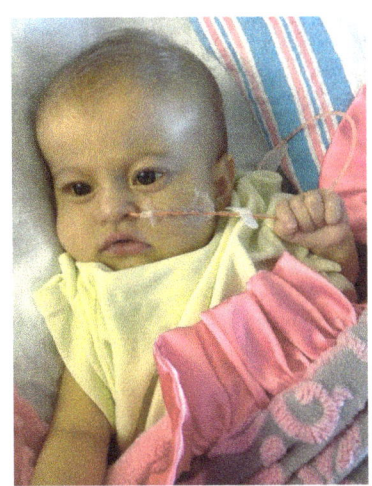

Sophia with her new feeding tube pre-transplant.

Sophia and Kayla the night Kayla shared that she was a match, and eight years later!

The night before transplant. Our last visit with Kayla. Kayla and Sophia had superhero capes made by Kayla.

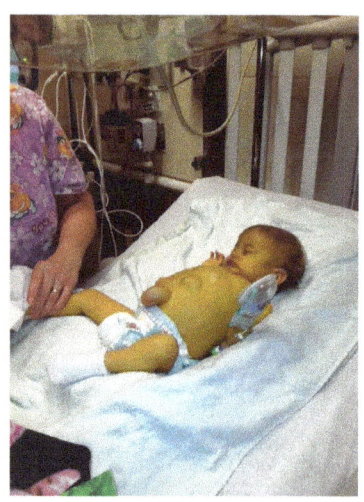

Sophia the night before transplant, getting an antibiotic bath. Her belly was so distended and she was in so much pain.

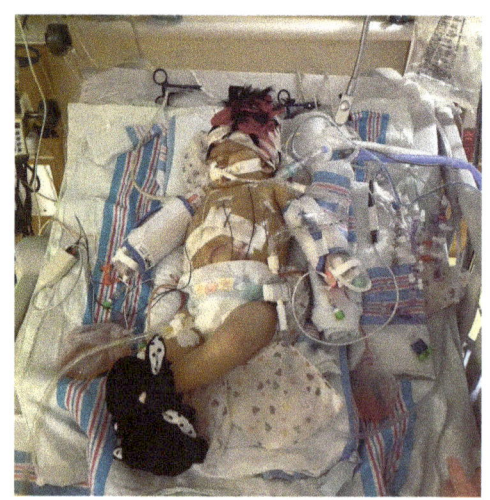

Sophia the day after transplant. I kept her looking stylish, even when sedated.

Sophia eight months post-transplant. She didn't skip a beat!

Sophioa and Kayla celebrating our Irish heritage in Chicago with the green river.

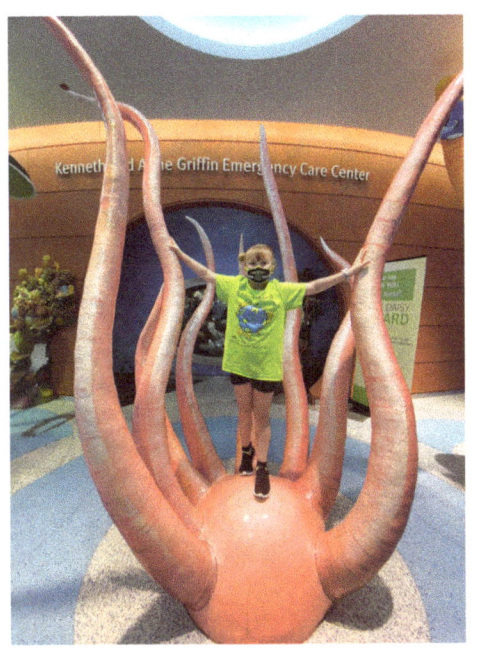

Sophia at her nine-year transplant clinic. She truly loves her team and hospital.

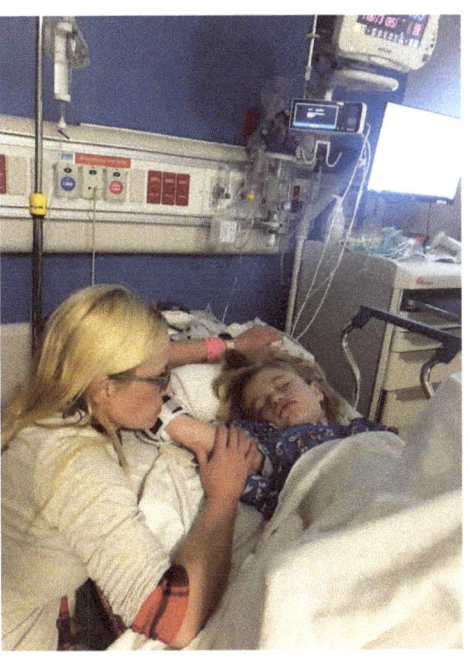

Sophia following a routine biopsy.

Sophia in 2022. She truly loves the simple parts of life.

Sophia with Daddy. She truly loves the outdoors.

Sophia, Kayla, and Stephanie family photos, 2022.

Skrede family photo, 2022, along with Kayla.
Kayla will always be our fifth child.

A Piece of Me Now Smiles Back at Me

By Beth Battista

I used to wonder what more I could do in this lifetime to make a difference. On June 19th, 2016, I found the answer. I had just finished my twelfth year of teaching and was enjoying a relaxing summer day at home. As I was scrolling through Facebook, I stopped when I saw my close friend and current co-teacher's headline that read: "Please read and share!" The attached post started with a plea: "**DONOR NEEDED: PLEASE SHARE**." As I continued to read, tears filled my eyes. My heart ached for this family, so I hoped that they would find the help they needed soon. Being a mother myself, I could hear the pain and desperation in this mom's voice. They needed a living kidney donor to save their four-year-old daughter's life. This reached deep into the depths of my soul, and I immediately called the number listed for the University of Wisconsin Health Transplant Center. Without hesitation, I told them I wanted to undergo testing to see if I could be a match for Lyla. This was an easy decision for me. I knew in my heart it was something I had to do. From that first phone call, I had no doubt in my mind that I would be Lyla's match.

At four years old, Lyla was diagnosed with a rare autoimmune disorder, microscopic polyangiitis (MPA), that caused her kidneys to fail. Lyla received daily peritoneal dialysis at home, which was effective in eliminating about 20–25% of the toxins from her frail little body. The leftover toxins, however, were damaging Lyla's heart and other organs, and long-term dialysis could have permanently damaged the lining of her abdomen. Lyla had a tube in her stomach and would spend ten to twelve hours a day hooked up to her dialysis machine. The dialysis also severely dehydrated her body, causing near-constant headaches, nausea, and muscle cramps. She could only drink one liter of water (the equivalent of four baby bottles) every twenty-four hours, because her kidneys could not process fluids. Imagine trying to tell a young child that they can't have something to drink. Lyla had a long road ahead of her, but if anyone could put up a fight against this terrible disease, it was her.

The potential donor process began with an initial thirty-minute phone health screening. During this time, blood type, family health history, and other health-related questions were asked. A few days later, they called me back to set up an appointment to have my blood samples taken: eighteen vials! The immunological tests would determine blood typing, cross-matching, and tissue typing, all of which are critical for finding the best match for transplantation. Wow! Things were really moving along. I sat down with my husband, Jason, to talk with him about what I was doing. He was extremely supportive and behind me 100%.

A week or so later, I received another phone call asking if I was still committed to the process, and if so, they wanted me to come to the hospital for a final round of testing. This was a full day of tests, including an EKG, a psychological evaluation, a chest X-ray, and a CT scan. While I was at UW Hospital, I met our incredible transplant coordinator, Beth, and my amazing surgeon, Dr. Redfield. I remember feeling a sense of calm as I walked out of the hospital that day. The transplant team had yet to approve me as Lyla's donor, but I already knew in my heart I would be. That same day, I also found out that Lyla was on my class list for the upcoming school year, which meant I would be her teacher!

The next week and a half was long. Oh, how I wanted to share the news with Lyla's family that I had gotten tested, but I knew I had to wait until I had final confirmation from the transplant team. During this time, I shared the news with my parents and a few close friends, all of whom supported my decision to become a living donor.

On Thursday, September 1st, 2016, while I was in the classroom teaching, I received the call that I had been approved to donate my kidney to Lyla! I remember feeling all kinds of emotions rushing through my body. I was now able to help this sweet child and give her a better life. I could also finally share the news with Lyla's family.

Lyla's mom, Dena, set up a meeting with myself and my co-teacher, Laura, to go over all of Lyla's medical needs in detail during the school day. Little did she know that Laura and I were planning on a sharing a BIG surprise! We anxiously waited for Dena to arrive. She sat down at the table and began to give us information about medication, water-intake limits, activity limitations, and a lot more. After hearing Dena explain Lyla's daily needs, Laura and I interjected and told her what a wonderful mother she was and how we knew she was doing everything imaginable to help her daughter. We then slid a small gift box across the table and told her she was incredible and that we had gotten her a gift. Dena's jaw dropped. "Seriously, I feel like I should be getting you guys presents. Should I open it now?" she asked. Dena unwrapped the box and began reading a small note that read "I may just be her teacher now, but soon a little piece of me will be with Lyla forever. I'm Lyla's kidney donor." Dena was in awe of the news she had read on this small piece of paper. "You are? Are you freaking kidding me!" We both got up and embraced each other. Happy tears streamed down our faces. This miracle had brought our two families together forever.

The next few weeks were a complete whirlwind. Dena asked if she could share the news with family and friends on social media, and the kind responses and the outpouring of love and support came in quickly. Our story was being shared over and over. Local news stations contacted me early the next morning, wanting interviews. We were overwhelmed, but in a good way. By sharing our story, we could also bring awareness to the need for living donors. After the local news stations aired our story, it continued to get picked up by other news outlets all over the country and the world. Our story had gone viral! I was a teacher, and being in the public eye was not something I was completely comfortable with, but the way this was traveling reassured me that if Lyla and I could help just one other person, then it was worth it. What an honor it was to have all of these famous and noteworthy people asking to speak with us. From the *Today Show*, to *ABC World News Tonight with David Muir*, to the BBC, to the biggest surprise of them all: In October of 2016, we were flown to Los Angeles to be on *The Ellen DeGeneres Show!*

What a once in a lifetime experience! It was truly amazing. Ellen surprised Lyla with a basket full of goodies related to her favorite Disney princess, Merida, from the movie *Brave*. In the movie, Merida talks about how being brave doesn't mean you're not scared, it means that you're scared but you do something anyway. This truly embodied what Lyla had been through and would continue to fight through over the next few months. I was also surprised by a guest appearance from my favorite football team's quarterback, Aaron Rodgers! He invited me and my family to a Green Bay Packers game, to come down to the field to meet him. This was an experience I could share with my kids, and something that they could enjoy and remember forever.

February 22nd, 2017, was confirmed as our surgery date. The months of waiting were finally over, and Lyla was admitted to the hospital two days before the transplant. She settled into her room and was even allowed a few visitors. The night before the surgery,

I took Lyla on an in-door wagon ride around the American Family Children's Hospital (AFCH), which is connected to the University of Wisconsin Health University Hospital.

I didn't get much sleep that night as I was anxiously awaiting transplant day. Early the next morning, I arrived at the hospital and began the check-in process. Lyla was also getting prepped for surgery since timing was critical for an optimal outcome. I gave hugs and kisses to my husband before I was wheeled off to the surgery room. Once in the operating room, I remember seeing huge lights and counting down from ten. The surgery started, and both families anxiously awaited any news. My surgery, which was laparoscopic, took place at the UW Hospital and lasted about four hours, while Lyla's was next door at AFCH. Since we were not in the same surgical area, once my kidney was removed, it was put in a special cooler and carried over to Lyla's operating room. Her *new* kidney was placed in her little body and immediately began doing its job. The transplant was a HUGE success!

The next day, I was able to visit Lyla and witness the gift of life in action. She could drink fluids again and didn't have dialysis tubes running out of her body. Over the next few months, Lyla continued to make tremendous strides in her recovery. She was growing like a weed and enjoying being a five-year-old.

My recovery went extremely well. I was discharged from the hospital forty-eight hours after the transplant and came home to so many kind-hearted notes, flowers, and treats. I had a huge support system and could not have recovered so quickly without them. I went back to work in my classroom four weeks later. It was incredible to be back with my students and to see their little, smiling faces again. I had missed them all so much!

Two months after surgery, Lyla was back at school. We were reunited in the classroom where we had first met. Both of us were able to finish out the academic year and enjoy 4K graduation together.

Seeing Lyla finish her preschool education and enjoy running and playing with her classmates was the best gift of all.

Lyla, her family, and I have remained close, and we celebrated our five-year transplant anniversary in February of 2022. We've spent holidays and vacations together, and we will continue to spread awareness for both organ donation and living organ donation. In 2018, we took part in a gala featuring singer-songwriter John Legend. This fundraiser was for American Family Children's Hospital. Dena and Lyla were presenters during the auction and were able to raise thousands of dollars that went directly to the ground-breaking research taking place at AFCH in Madison. Another charity near and dear to our hearts is Make-A-Wish. Lyla had her wish granted, and she and her family enjoyed the trip of a lifetime at Walt Disney World in Orlando. In 2020, Dena hosted an incredible fortieth birthday party for me. The theme was "A Night in Vegas." People played games and donated winnings to help us reach our goal of granting two special wishes to deserving kids in Wisconsin. We were able to raise over $12,000 in one night!

Because of organ donation, Lyla and I will be forever bonded. We hope our story continues to help inspire others to always be kind to one another and to live life to the fullest.

While I was teaching second and third grades, we had the honor of having Brenda Cortez do a virtual author visit with the class. The children were introduced to Howl the Owl® and Brenda read one of her books to us. Each child also colored their own special picture of Howl. They learned about kindness and the importance of helping others who are in need.

About Beth

Beth Battista was born and raised in Madison, Wisconsin. She grew up with two older sisters, Amy and Lori. Her parents, Bill and

Alice, were high-school sweethearts and moved from Pennsylvania to Wisconsin so her dad could attend graduate school at the University of Wisconsin-Madison. Beth attended Madison West High School and graduated from Edgewood College with a degree in elementary education in 2003. She began her teaching career at a private preschool, where she taught kindergarten for four-year-olds.

Beth is married and has two children. Her family keeps her busy on most weekends as she finds herself at the hockey rink, basketball court, or football field. Beth also has two rescue doggies and is a strong advocate for adopting a shelter pet. She is a huge Green Bay Packers and Wisconsin Badgers fan. After eighteen years of teaching, Beth decided to try something new and is currently working in the Business Services Department at the University of Wisconsin-Madison.

You can connect with Beth on social media: Facebook and Instagram.

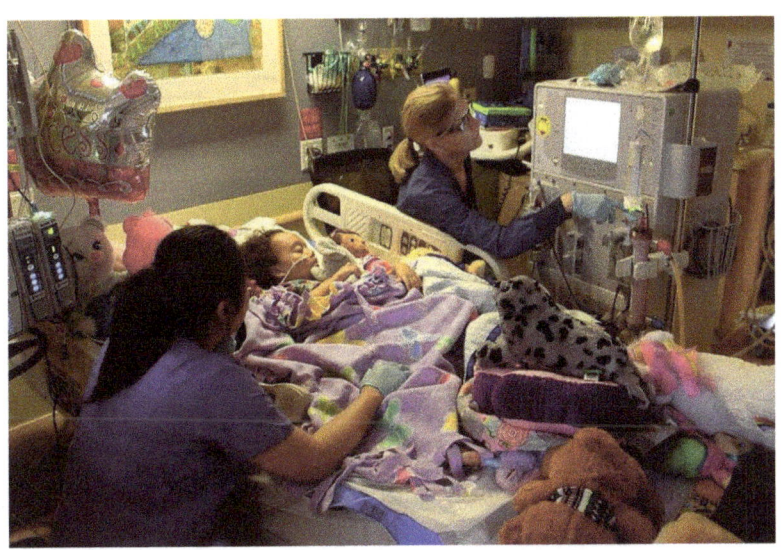

Lyla at the American Family Children's Hospital after being rushed to the ER.

The note I surprised Lyla's Mom Dena with sharing the news that I was approved to be her donor.

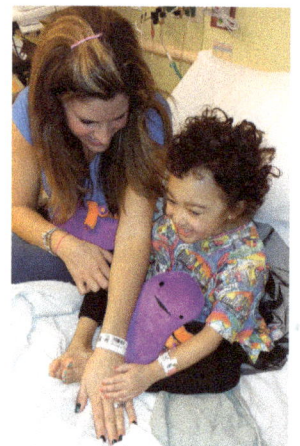

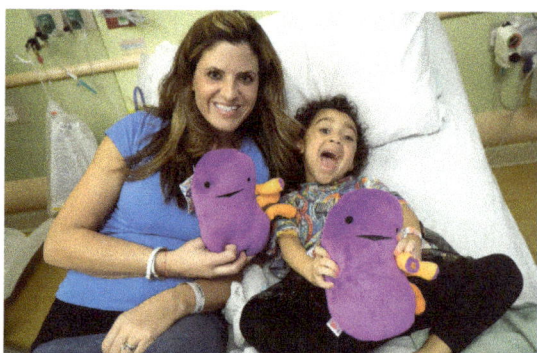

Kidney buddies for life the night before the transplant

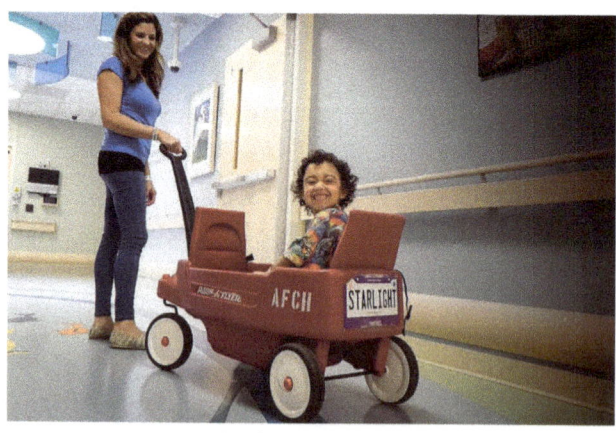

Wagon ride the night before surgery.

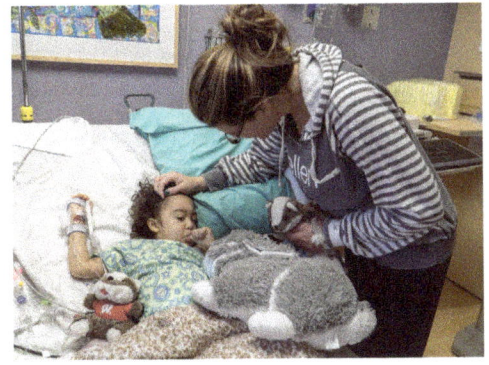

Brenda Cortez and HOWL
the OWL® make a virtual
author visit to our class.

Welcoming Lyla back to school.

4-year-old Kindergarten
graduation day.

At the Ellen Show.

*My family's visit to the Packers game
and picture with Aaron Rodgers.*

Celebrating 6 months after the transplant on vacation together.

American Family Children's Hospital Gala Fundraiser .

A Father's Gift

By Stephanie Mullett

In September 2017, our family of three was blessed with the arrival of our teeny-tiny, baby boy, Bryce. Due to complications in utero, labor was induced at thirty-two weeks. At the time of his birth, Bryce weighed a mere 3 pounds, 1 ounce, and he was 14 inches long. When curled up, like most newborns, he could fit neatly into a rectangular tissue box. After birth, he was immediately taken to the NICU where he spent twenty-eight days before being discharged home.

After learning there was something concerning with Bryce's heart development at the twenty-week anatomy scan, weekly appointments with specialists, which left us with more questions than answers, became the new reality for our family. The doctors tried their best to explain the reality of Bryce's heart being under extreme pressure in utero, and the potential complications of a premature birth. Within the first forty-eight hours of Bryce's life, his suspected diagnosis took a major turn, from hypoplastic left heart syndrome to a rare genetic disorder called *Alagille syndrome*. The latter quickly became the top topic in our online searches as my husband, Andrew, and I scoured the internet for any information to answer our ever-growing list of questions. We learned that Alagille syndrome effects about one in 30,000–50,000 individuals in the world, and the impact of the mutation in his genes could be categorized as "no concerns" or "mild," to the more severe complications that may include a variety of surgeries, an organ transplant, or pre-adulthood death. Some of the most substantial aspects of Alagille syndrome include the lifelong challenge to gain adequate weight, uncontrollable and debilitating itching, complications during procedures due to multiple abnormal organ systems, and the overarching anxiety of the unknown, as this rare disease has not been extensively researched or studied by specialists.

While Bryce was being admitted to the NICU, we were introduced to a new team of doctors who would be driving his plan of care. He would routinely see a hepatologist to track his liver function, a nephrologist for his small, underdeveloped kidneys, a cardiologist to continue monitoring his heart, and a neurologist for his brain. We learned that Alagille syndrome (ALGS) carries a higher risk for the development of aneurysms in patients. The team recommended Bryce have genetic testing done to fully determine the genetic mutation on the JAG1 or NOTCH2 genes, both of which are associated with Alagille syndrome. Receiving a genetic confirmation does not change the plan of care, but what it can confirm may be helpful for future family planning or research regarding Bryce. In November 2017, the geneticist met with us and confirmed that Bryce did indeed have Alagille syndrome, and that given my medical history and other characteristics, such as a heart murmur, challenges gaining weight as a young child, and facial characteristics, I too probably had ALGS. At the time I was twenty-seven, and even though I had never had any significant health issues, this concern did have future implications regarding whether or not I could be a potential organ donor for Bryce.

As we adjusted to our new life at home with a premature baby, Bryce continued to need constant oxygen support, as well as supplemental calories mixed in with breast milk to encourage weight gain. The next few months were sleepless, stressful, yet overall hopeful that perhaps Bryce would be within the realm of mild impact with his disorder. We were told the data at the time suggested that if a child with Alagille syndrome could make it to their first birthday with their native liver, the better the chances they would make it to adulthood.

At the start of 2018, new concerns with Bryce's health began emerging. He was frequently vomiting after feedings, and despite our best efforts, he was struggling to gain weight. This was a significant concern, as it could impact brain development and growth. When Bryce was five-months-old, his hepatologist recommended having an NG tube placed to increase caloric intake and promote weight gain. Our sleepless nights dramatically increased, and due to the amount of profuse vomiting, our washing machine and dryer were constantly running to keep up with the never-ending pile of towels, blankets, and spoiled clothing. With this medical intervention, Bryce was able to gain about half a pound of weight within a month, but coupled with his deteriorating liver numbers, his team became increasingly concerned that he would need a liver transplant in the near future. Due to his extremely small size, the possible complications that could arise during transplant were substantially increased.

At six-months-old, in March 2018, Bryce spent a week in the hospital to have a Broviac port placed intravenously. He also had a transplant evaluation completed by his team during this time. Medication was not supporting Bryce's deteriorating liver, and given the diagnosis of ALGS, we knew that complications would continue to progress and most likely become life-threatening. Hearing the words that our son, our tiny peanut, would require a lifesaving organ transplant was devastating. This was unchartered territory for our entire family, and most days, the anxiety and fear of what may come was suffocating. In addition, before Bryce could become eligible to be placed on the national transplant list, he would need a heart catheterization procedure to place pulmonary stents in his arteries. While we were waiting for this procedure, which was rescheduled once after Bryce was hospitalized for having the flu and another time after his Broviac broke, Andrew and I began notifying friends and family. We let them know that our sweet boy needed a liver, which could come from either a deceased donor or a living donor.

At the end of May 2018, Bryce was officially listed for a liver transplant. His PELD score quickly jumped from a sixteen to a thirty-two after his team submitted a request for extra points due to extreme weight deficiency and uncontrollable pruritus, which is an intense and debilitating itch due to elevated bile salts. A PELD score is a scoring system for children with pediatric end-stage liver disease that helps determine the order of who receives a liver transplant. The higher the score, the sicker the child. Shortly after, Andrew was notified that he was a blood match for Bryce, so he began the necessary testing to explore his ability to become Bryce's liver donor.

As the days passed, the collective planning and anxiety within our family kicked into overdrive. Overwhelming thoughts of *when would we get the call, would the call come in time to save Bryce's life, and would he survive the surgery* dictated our days. Then there were questions of who would watch our almost seven-year-old daughter while we were over an hour away from home for an expected two to four weeks post-transplant, and how would we ensure that both of our children felt loved, supported, and stable. All of this kept me up many nights. For my own sanity, I changed the ringtones on my phone so that when the hospital called, I would know immediately, instead of experiencing an extreme mix of emotions each time my phone rang.

The days passed in a foggy blur. Bryce started experiencing even more complications from his failing liver. He was in and out of the hospital due to significant bloody stools, sometimes requiring blood transfusions. It was during this time that we also set up in-home physical therapy to support his developmental delays in gross motor skills. From the time of Bryce's birth and up to this point, Andrew and I had both left our respective careers and could not comprehend what our future would look like.

On the morning of June 14th, we received the call we had been holding our breath for. A liver had become available for Bryce. His team advised us to start packing our bags because we needed to report to the hospital in six hours! As we quickly executed our detailed plan of action, I felt like we were trying to squeeze in a months' worth of future experiences into a few hours. We picked up our daughter's favorite lunch, had a picnic outside, took as many family pictures as possible, notified every family member and friend we could think of, and attempted to pack everything we envisioned we would potentially need for a month away from home. Throughout the chaos of the day, our hearts were heavy with the realization that, somewhere out there, another family was having to say goodbye to their loved one and had made the ultimate sacrifice to donate their organs. Our joy was directly tied to their despair, and that was a hard burden to acknowledge.

An hour before we were set to leave for the hospital, my phone rang with the special hospital ringtone. The team had to make the difficult decision to turn down the organ due to concern for disease transmission. My heart was absolutely shattered. Our son wasn't going to receive the gift of life, but I could only imagine the emotions that the donor family was experiencing. June 14th will always hold a special spot in our transplant journey as the day someone very important lost their life, the day their family was willing to explore the options of organ donation even in their darkest moments.

July rolled around, and our lives continued in a whirlwind of scheduled appointments and therapies, medicine administration, nightly changes of intravenous TPN (total parenteral nutrition) and lipids, unexpected hospitalizations, and the daily acknowledgement that Bryce's liver was continuing to get worse with no end in sight. Andrew continued to complete a barrage of required testing, labs, and imaging to see if he was a viable candidate, and as per usual, we were in a constant state of "hurry up and wait" for the next requirement. In addition, I had started a new position with a non-profit in our area and felt an odd sense of taking on a new opportunity, knowing full well that when we got *the call*, I would have to drop everything and attend to my son's health.

Near the end of the month, as we sat at our home away from home at the hospital for the umpteenth in-patient stay due to excessive and continuous blood in Bryce's stool, Andrew took a quick phone call. When he hung up, he asked me if we had any plans for August 7th, which was about eleven days away. Perplexed, I looked at him and laughed because he knew that we were living our lives day by day and that I was lucky to have definitive plans for an hour away, much less a week and a half away. He announced that all necessary tests were reviewed, and the teams at both the adult hospital and the children's hospital had decided that he was a viable match to be Bryce's live liver donor. We finally had our date set! We just needed Bryce and Andrew to stay healthy enough to make it to transplant day.

After the initial elation of knowing Bryce was one step closer to getting his new liver, the anxiety of having both Andrew and Bryce in-patient and recovering from surgery at the same time came crashing down. An added layer of managing all the moving pieces became evident, and thankfully, our families stepped up immediately to support us in any way possible. Duties were assigned to my mom, dad, aunt, mother-in-law, sister, and brothers-in-law, and even a few close neighbors to hopefully cover all of the bases and to keep our daughter safe and well loved while Andrew focused on recovery and I focused on supporting Bryce and Andrew as best as possible.

After three weeks at my new job, I walked away with the expectation that I would come back whenever I was able to, however long that may take. In addition, we had our daughter's seventh birthday party planned two days prior to transplant day, and with the support and care of our team, she was able to have a special day centered around her, living life as a regular kid. The intertwinement of joyous occasions and moments with the constant battle of concern, fear, and sadness had created a web of emotions and memories that allowed us to reflect with happiness on the journey.

Early on the morning of August 7th, 2018, I met Andrew and his mom across the street in the adult hospital OR waiting room for a quick hug and a kiss before he calmly entered his stage of the process. I then returned to the children's hospital where my mom, daughter, and aunt were showering Bryce with kisses and taking as many pictures as possible. Before long, we walked down to the OR, changed Bryce into his familiar dog print children's gown, gave him one last kiss that I prayed would cover him in safety and comfort, and handed him off to the waiting nurses. Two of the most important people in my life were now at the mercy of modern medicine and their capable teams. Everything was out of my hands and out of my control. Despite this, the entire day was met with a sense of peace surrounding our little group, as we anxiously sat in the waiting area we had claimed as our base camp. My daughter enjoyed the day, receiving copious amounts of love and entertainment from our attending family members. She also got to spend some time with the Denver Broncos Cheerleaders, who happened to be visiting the hospital that day.

Bryce's incredible surgeons, Dr. Wachs and Dr. Adams, would nonchalantly exit the operating room every so often and personally update us on the status of Bryce's procedure. As I reminded them frequently that day, I wanted this surgery to be the most boring surgery of their careers: nothing special or exciting, nothing they would feel the need to document in their future career notes. We simply wanted a straightforward, uncomplicated, by-the-book procedure, with an uninteresting post-surgical recovery. Andrew's surgical team at the hospital across the street kept us updated with his progress, and oddly, we kept a close eye on the main doors to see if we could spot the organ carrier delivering his section of liver to be placed in Bryce. By late afternoon, Andrew was out of surgery and beginning his recovery in the ICU. As he slowly regained consciousness, he groggily requested a visit from a cheerleader, rather than from the attending nurse or his eager wife.

Bryce's team proceeded with the transplant, and after eleven hours, his abdomen was sewn up and he was transferred to the PICU. The surgery was a success, the new liver was in, and the team was optimistic about not needing to return to the operating room to address any post-surgical complications. When I was finally able to kiss Bryce's sweet body as he lay on the bed covered in wires and tubes, and with new incisions to mark his journey, I was overcome with more emotions than I could process. He had made it through the surgery and had the new liver that his body so desperately needed.

The post-surgical recovery of Bryce's body was nothing short of miraculous. On day two, he was extubated, and by day three, I was able to pick him up and hold him in my arms. Andrew made progress towards recovery as well but met with a few unexpected complications. His digestive system struggled to restart, but with some changes in his medications and a lot of hard work, he finally turned a corner. On day nine post-transplant, Andrew was discharged from the hospital, so we wheeled his wheelchair across the well-known path, and he was able to visit his son for the first time.

By day fourteen, Bryce was discharged from the hospital, and for the first time in over two weeks, our family, all four of us, were back home sleeping in our own beds. Both Andrew and Bryce had an extensive medication regimen that had to be managed multiple times a day, plus we had to navigate the typical post-surgical physical stay. He had his port removed, as it was unnecessary as this point due to his healthy liver absorbing fats and nutrients at the appropriate rate. Our recovery journey post-transplant was busy, with a slow decrease in appointments, lab draws and ultrasounds, until a short time later when we noticed we were finally spending more time at home rather than in a hospital. After the initial shock of what we had been through passed, we began to rebuild our lives and attempt to move forward, physically, emotionally, and financially.

As we approach our fourth "transplantiversary," I am still in complete awe of the lifesaving gift that Andrew was able to provide for our son, Bryce. Bryce is a thriving, growing, incredible little kid, who enjoys playing video games, jumping on the trampoline, and spreading joy and laughter to those around him with his silly antics. The liver transplant did not entirely fix Bryce, as he still struggles with other complications due to the underlying disorder of Alagille syndrome. In addition, concerns with post-transplant health are constant, including the fact that Bryce's immune suppressants keep him at a higher risk for contracting other common illnesses. Navigating the pandemic for the last two years has been a struggle, as we have had to constantly weigh the safety of Bryce's health, while attempting to expand his environment to include school and peers.

Bryce also still struggles with his feeding development and eating enough calories to support appropriate growth. In November 2021, his team, as well as Andrew and I, felt that it was in Bryce's best interest to have a G-tube placed to allow us to give him more calories day and night. He is doing both physical therapy and feeding therapy in hopes of helping to close some of his developmental gaps. He also struggles, as all members in our family do, to process the psychosocial and emotional ramifications of what the early years of his life have entailed.

We are grateful for each day Bryce has been given because of his special gift from Andrew. We are forever appreciative of each and every surgeon, physician, nurse, nursing assistant, coordinator, therapist, and hospital custodian who took the time to care for Andrew and Bryce throughout their procedures and recoveries. Our sweet little peanut, Bryce, would most definitely not be alive today had he not been given a second chance at life through organ donation. Because of organ donation, my husband was able to save our son.

I would like to thank our family and friends for their never-ending support and love through all of the ups and downs. I would also like to thank Bryce's extensive team of incredible doctors and nurses at Children's Hospital Colorado, especially Dr. Amy Feldman, Dr. Megan Adams, and Transplant Coordinator, Lauren Pratscher, who have always answered my crazy questions without judgment and helped me feel educated and empowered throughout this journey. A big thank you to the Alagille Syndrome Alliance for helping us find resources, information, and our rare disease community. Lastly, I would like to thank my husband, Andrew, for being my rock and for saving Bryce's life.

About Stephanie

Stephanie lives in Colorado with her husband, Andrew, their two children, Emma and Bryce, and their dog, Bentley. Her professional background is in early childhood special education, and she hopes to continue to support, through education and advocacy, the community of those affected by Alagille syndrome.

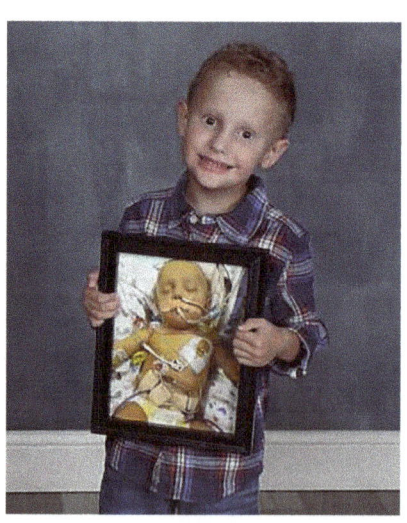

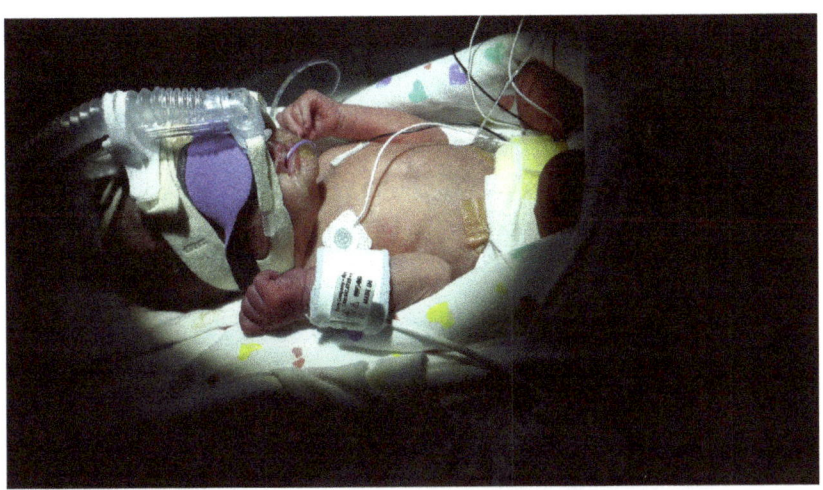

Bryce spent 28 days in the NICU after birth.

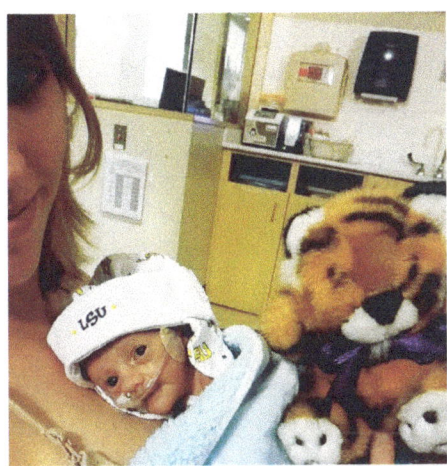

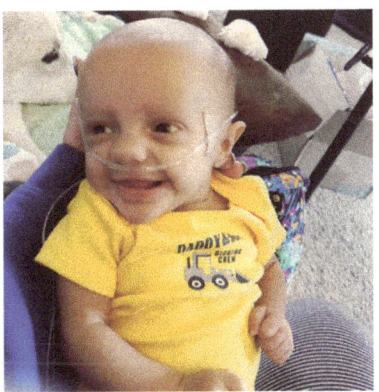

Bryce watched his first LSU football game in the NICU. He had to have been the tiniest fan that season.

Bryce was a very smiley baby, and brought so much joy to everyone around him.

Emma (6), Bryce (7 months old) celebrating Easter 2018. Bryce was severely jaundiced due to his failing liver.

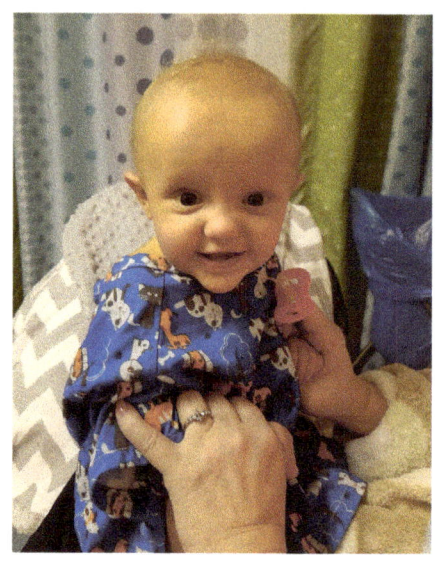

May 2018, Bryce had his first heart catheter procedure to place stents in his pulmonary arteries in preparation for his liver transplant.

Pruritus, or severe itching, is one of the most challenging symptoms of Alagille Syndrome. We frequently woke up in the morning to Bryce's crib being covered in blood from him itching through the night.

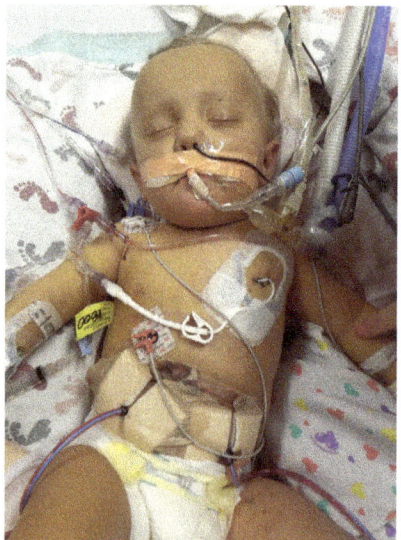

Bryce's transplant was on August 7th, 2018. He received a part of his dad's liver. This was the first time I was able to see Bryce after his surgery. Andrew didn't get to see him in person until 9 days later when Andrew was released from the hospital.

This was our first family photo post transplant. Our family has been through so much in the last five years, but we hold on to our love and laughter to get through the hard times.

Bryce and Andrew's first transplant anniversary. Bryce had a "piece" of Andrew's pizza :)

Bryce has always loved to play outside and enjoy the sunshine.

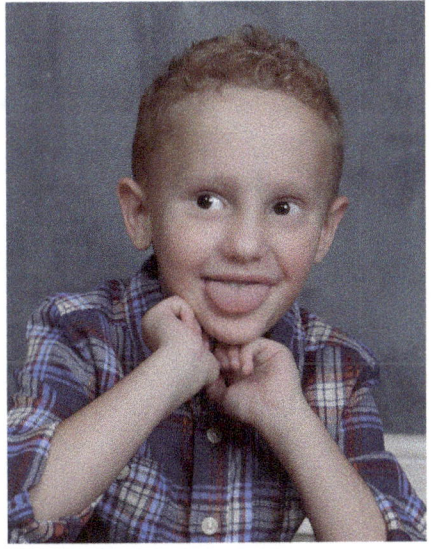

Bryce has quite the mischievous personality, and makes us all laugh with the silly things he says.

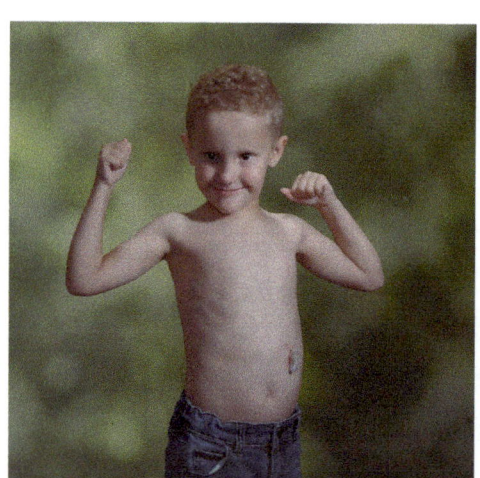

Bryce likes to show off his muscles any chance he can! He is one of the strongest kiddos I know.

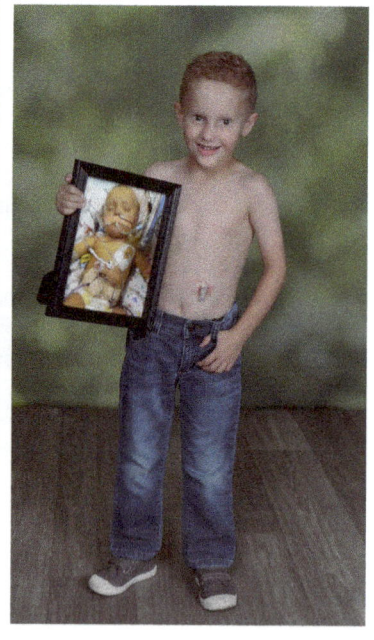

Pediatric Transplant: An Unexpected Journey

By John Welch

In the spring of 2000, my son, Austin, was two years old and had become ill with what at first seemed like the flu. He grew lethargic and was unable to hold down food or fluids for a couple of weeks. In an effort to determine what was wrong, my wife, Kelly, took Austin for multiple visits to the pediatrician, which usually resulted in lab work with negative results.

On June 1st of that year, Austin's pediatrician again ordered lab work at our local hospital. On the way to the car after the blood draw, Austin stumbled and fell. Kelly had to carry him the rest of the way to the car. During the drive home, Kelly realized that Austin's right arm was moving in an unusual motion, so she turned the car around and went back to the pediatrician's office for evaluation. Austin was immediately rushed to the emergency room, where they quickly determined they were not able to treat him. At this point, Austin was transported by ambulance to Doernbecher Children's Hospital in Portland, roughly fifty miles north.

While in the pediatric ICU, the staff determined that Austin had contracted E. coli, which had progressed to hemolytic uremic syndrome (HUS), which only occurs in ten percent of E. coli cases (primarily in young children and the elderly). Further testing showed that Austin was in complete renal failure and had suffered a large stroke as a result of the HUS. The doctors immediately placed Austin on hemodialysis to do the work of his kidney function. They also placed him in a medically induced coma so his medical team could treat the seizures that were being caused by the stroke.

After several days of observation, Austin's doctors felt that he had stabilized neurologically, and he was brought out of the coma. His kidney function, though, did not return as hoped. Austin remained in the hospital until near the end of August, so he could continue to be monitored neurologically and provided on-site dialysis and occupational therapy for issues caused by the stroke. Fortunately, Kelly was able to stay with him on a continuous basis to provide parental support.

Near the end of August, Austin was released from the hospital to return home; however, Kelly had to drive him to Portland three times a week for on-site dialysis, as there was no pediatric dialysis available in Salem.

Eventually, Kelly received training on how to utilize a peritoneal dialysis unit for home use. Austin had had minor surgery so he could be implanted with what amounted to filters, and he was able to continue with this type of dialysis at home for several months. Dialysis was performed every night during bedtime, which allowed him more normal juvenile activities during the day.

During this time, it was determined that Austin would not regain kidney function, and the conversation turned to renal transplant. Both Kelly and I were tested for compatibility, and through a complete stroke of good fortune, we both turned out to be good candidates for donating a kidney to Austin. At this point, we were each evaluated for kidney size, as we had to consider Austin's much smaller body. Kelly was selected to be the donor, as her kidney was small enough to be placed into Austin in a relatively short time period.

Austin was a bit too small still for an immediate transplant, so he was prescribed growth hormones to jump start his natural growth. This lasted until medical staff decided that the transplant could take place.

On July 16th, 2001, Austin received his transplant at Doernbecher Children's Hospital. Kelly, as an adult, had her kidney removed at Oregon Health & Science University, which is affiliated with Doernbecher and on the same campus as the children's hospital. While each recuperated in their individual hospital, I, caregiver to both, spent several days going back and forth between the two since they were each awake at different times.

Ten days post-surgery, after it was clear that the transplant was a success and there were no signs of rejection, we were able to bring Austin home. As weeks turned into months, post-transplant care became routine, if not second nature, for us. Immunosuppressant medications were taken religiously, along with proper hydration. Monthly renal function labs were also done, sometimes resulting in medication adjustments.

Austin's independent nature soon made its first appearance. He clearly preferred to be with kids (even if they were older than him) and had no issue with the idea of not telling Mom and Dad that he was headed out to be with the neighborhood kids. It has become a family joke that Austin was able to sneak out of our apartment and go to the community pool to be with the teenagers.

Within a number of years, as Austin grew older, he was progressively given more responsibility for his own self-care. By middle-school age, Austin was, for the most part, self-administering his medications according to his schedule, as well as keeping up with his fluid-intake requirements. School often made it challenging for Austin to maintain his high fluid-intake requirement, as staff sometimes felt that it was either not necessary or that it was disruptive to the classroom environment.

During the middle-school years, Austin often experienced a level of frustration with his physical education teachers, who would keep him out of certain activities such as flag football. Although he had a kidney guard that he wore for such activities, his teachers were not usually willing to take on the perceived risk of injury. This didn't sit well with Austin, who by this point was developing an interest in being involved in activities, especially sports.

In an attempt to be involved in some sort of sport, Austin tried out for his middle school track team. While not outstanding at the sport, the experience certainly helped with developing his willingness to try new challenges, especially those which others may have perceived as too dangerous or unattainable. To this day, Austin rarely asks others for their opinion regarding his desire to try new things; he simply goes out and starts the process.

During this period, Austin was introduced to Special Olympics. He qualified because of his stroke, which had caused certain learning delays. Austin often takes longer to learn school subjects and usually needs assistance, such as one-on-one services. Track and basketball were Austin's sports of choice. Kelly and I were then introduced to Austin's "no holds barred" attitude, which we continue to see to this day. Austin has the attitude of a go-getter in all fields that he has an interest in, whether it be sports, work, or his social environment.

To this day, Austin participates in the Transplant Games, an event designed for transplant patients, donors, and families that is held every two years. The Games absolutely showcase the success of transplants in general, especially for Austin.

After graduating from high school, Austin was ready for the next big step in life: getting a job and earning money. He knew that having his own money would be his first step towards independence from Mom and Dad. Austin was excited, but this was a bit scary for us.

After a short search, Austin was able to land his first job at Meals on Wheels. This job turned out to be perfect for him. He was able to get himself up early in the morning and plan his medication schedule.

He rode the bus to work, completed his workday, and rode the bus back home, completely on his own. This was big considering where Austin was at some twenty years previously – fighting to survive.

Today, at twenty-four, Austin seems years ahead of his peers in many aspects. His own health care is of upmost importance to him; maintaining a healthy, balanced lifestyle, scheduling and maintaining medical appointments, following prescribed immunosuppressant medication schedules, and watching his diet are all part of the life of a transplant patient.

For a transplant patient, there is a huge level of responsibility for taking care of yourself, and Austin has done remarkably well adapting to that. He has literally grown up with this responsibility, and it is second nature to him. He is in tune with the idea that his own health comes second to none when it comes to other outside influences.

For the last several years, Austin has been involved with Northwest Kidney Kids, a nonprofit organization based in Portland. He participated in their programs as a youth. Northwest Kidney Kids actively engages children who have, or need, kidney transplants, offering multiple outlets for them. Today, Austin volunteers in their fundraising programs. He is well aware of the organizations and programs of his youth, and he works to support them as an adult.

Kelly did remarkably well post-kidney donation. After several weeks of recuperation, she was able to return to a full, normal lifestyle, including walking in an organized half marathon a few years later.

As a stay-at-home parent, Kelly took on responsibilities that few parents are tasked with. Being the parent of a medically fragile child requires a level of responsibility above normal parenting. Kelly has been the point-person for Austin's medical needs, especially in the early years post-transplant. She was the one working with the medical staff regarding Austin's medical needs and ensuring that he followed transplant protocols.

Since Austin and his care was the center of our world, especially Kelly's, when he moved out on his own, it was an adjustment for us as parents. At times, it was a bit of a struggle. Letting go of parental responsibilities after all those years and letting him have full control of his medical needs was not easy.

As a family, we participate in the Transplant Games. Austin competes as an organ recipient, and Kelly participates as a donor. This truly showcases the success of organ/tissue transplantation. It also allows us to discuss the topic in the workplace, creating an open door for the importance of organ and tissue transplantation. We are able to explain the premise of the Transplants Games as well as promote the idea that transplant patients are able to return to a normal lifestyle. With my position in public transit, and Kelly's position in home health care, we find that we have a wide and varied audience interested in the subject.

As I creep towards retirement, I find myself increasingly occupied with nonprofit campaigns geared towards the transplant theme. In 2008, I was invited to be involved in the ground-breaking efforts in launching Transplants in Action (TIA), based in Salem, Oregon. This organization is dedicated to educating local residents about the great need for organ and tissue transplants. I currently serve as President of Transplants in Action and am actively restructuring the organization and implementing new avenues for outreach. I have been able to bring on an entirely new board (all of whom are outside the transplant community) as well as attend local outreach events (such as the local Kroc Center Family Health Fair) designed to increase awareness of what tissue and organs can be donated.

In addition, I also volunteer with Donate Life Northwest and The National Kidney Foundation, all in an effort to be involved at the local, regional, and national level. Kelly has also volunteered on an as-needed basis with Donate Life Northwest.

About John

Born in Pasadena, California, John moved with his family to Oregon in the late 1960s, settling in Salem in 1973. Nestled in the Willamette Valley, John considers this to be home. After graduating from high school in Salem, John attended Chemeketa before serving in the U.S. Air Force in Washington, Texas, and Germany. Today, John is employed by Salem Area Mass Transit, operating transit buses over fixed routes within the urban growth boundary. In addition, John also trains new hires to help them obtain their CDL licenses and learn how to operate transit buses.

Austin and Kelly at the 2022 Transplant Games in San Diego.

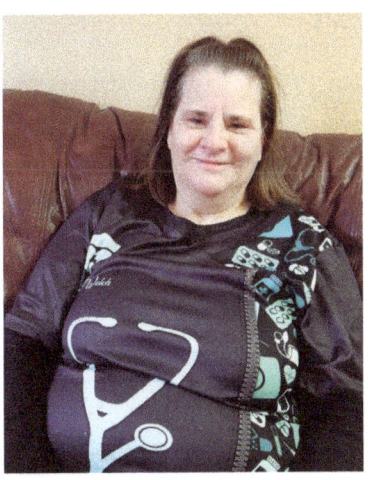

Austin advocating in DC

"Deeder"
Our Superhero Son!
By Dan Richardson

In Loving Memory of Dylan Richardson
(May 11ᵗʰ, 2000 – July 13ᵗʰ, 2007)

Our family nickname for Dylan was "Deeder." When learning words as a baby, he would often say, "Deeder, deeder, deeder." I do not recall what he was trying to say, but I thought it was so precious. I often asked him to repeat it, and from there, it somehow evolved into his nickname. We still refer to him by it today.

Dylan was a very smart boy for his age. He excelled in school and participated in accelerated classes. He was exceptional at reading. His favorite, the Magic Tree House series, brought adventures and suspense that he could not get enough of. His creative side was apparent in the pictures he drew, or notes and letters that he was just learning to write. Dylan loved Spiderman, SpongeBob, and Star Wars. He enjoyed baseball, light saber fights, and riding his bike. Playing with friends, hanging out with Mom and Dad, and pestering his brothers and their friends were also high on Dylan's to-do list. He also became incredibly good at Guitar Hero. So good, in fact, that he beat grown men! He liked playing I Spy and had boundless amounts of energy at any park. That is, until the ice cream truck arrived!

Dylan loved stuffed animals, and upon receiving each one, his first priority was to give it a special name. His favorite was a black-and-white puppy, given to him by his aunt, which he named Jake. In silly moments, he was an expert at armpit farts! It always made me laugh! To put it simply, Dylan was a good boy, and we miss him dearly.

Dylan's superhero story began on Wednesday afternoon, July 11th, 2007.

The Phone Call

It was a routine late Wednesday afternoon at work. I was very busy and working long hours. It was after 5:00 pm when my phone rang, and I saw a local number I didn't recognize on the caller ID. Since it was after hours, I figured it was a wrong number and when they heard my voice message, they would realize it and hang up. Like we've all done, I let the call go to voicemail. I didn't think much of it.

The message light then came on, and I remember raising my eyebrow a little bit. Fifteen minutes or so went by before I decided to listen to the message. The message was from a man and started like any typical message: "Hello, my name is..." (I can't recall his name). He continued with, "I'm calling on behalf of your wife. She and your son were in an accident. Everything seems to be OK, but your son appears to be injured. Please call me back as soon as possible." Needless to say, I called him right back. He was very calm while speaking. I questioned him in order to gauge the severity of the accident. "Are they hurt? How bad?" And so on. His description of the scene led me to believe that the accident wasn't that serious.

I hung up and wondered briefly which one of my boys he was referring to. I immediately called home, hoping to catch one of the other boys there. Thankfully, Nick (our 17-year-old) answered, and he told me that both he and Bryan (our 14-year-old) were home. Instantly, I knew who was with my wife, Lisa; it was Dylan, our seven-year-old son. I told Nick that Mom and Dylan were in an accident and it didn't sound serious, but they were being taken to the hospital. I told the boys to go to the scene, take pictures of our minivan, and meet me at the hospital. I finished things up at work as quickly as I could and got up to leave. I told a couple of co-workers that my wife and son were in an accident and that I had to go. My work would have to wait until the next morning.

Arriving at the Hospital

I arrived at Mercy Hospital in Aurora, Illinois. Upon arriving, I remember security people beginning to clear the area outside the emergency room as a helicopter was due in soon. Once inside, I was brought to the emergency room where Dylan was. I could see him, and they let me get close to him while the team continued to work on him. I could see the severe gash on the side of his face, his lower lip hanging down and his head still caged in head gear. A nurse informed me that he had a broken leg and had hit his head pretty hard. So hard, in fact, that they had drugged him into forced unconsciousness and were prepping him for transportation to another hospital, where they could take "better care of him."

"Where is Dylan going?" I asked. *Lutheran General Hospital in Park Ridge, Illinois*, they told me. This was when I found out that security was clearing the area for a helicopter to take Dylan. I asked if I could go with him, but they said there was no room. Everything was happening so fast. My life was normal and routine, and now this. My attention turned to Lisa. She was in another room, and she was hurt, but not seriously. She was lying on a gurney, her head still restrained, with a nurse on each side. Upon reaching her, the very first thing she asked was, "He's hurt pretty bad, isn't he?" I said yes and told her they were taking him somewhere else. Lisa described the accident to me. Our minivan was broadsided. The impact caused the van to flip over and land upright. Dylan took the brunt of the impact. He was sitting in the back on the passenger side, right at the point of the impact. Lisa was not yet cleared to get up before it was time for Dylan to leave, so they wheeled her gurney over to see him before he left for the helicopter ride that he would not be awake to remember.

Watching Dylan leave in the helicopter, and not being able to be with him, was the most excruciatingly difficult experience I had ever faced up to that time. The team at Mercy suggested I head over to Lutheran General to be with him. Unfortunately, Lisa wasn't going to be released for a while, so I had to decide to stay with her, or go. Our next-door neighbor, an Aurora police officer, arrived at some point during the chaos. He had heard about the accident over the radio. He graciously drove me to Lutheran General. It seemed like it took forever to get there. When we arrived, we were taken to a room off of the emergency department. We waited. Finally, a nurse came in and told us Dylan was in surgery, and we could wait upstairs on the second floor where he would eventually be taken. We waited some more. I think it was after 11:00 pm by the time the neurosurgeon came out to speak with me. He said Dylan's head was hurt very badly and his brain was swelling. The swelling was so bad, that he had to remove part of Dylan's skull in order give his brain more room. He also told me that, due to the severity of the brain injury, they were not going to address his other injuries, his broken leg, or gashed face at that time. I asked if Dylan would be all right. The doctor couldn't, or rather wouldn't, say. He could only tell me, *Time will tell.*

Lisa and the boys finally arrived. After another wait, we were finally allowed to see Dylan. It was after midnight by this time. He was in a coma, his head wrapped in a gauze helmet, and he had every tube and instrument imaginable hooked up to him. He could not breathe on his own and was on a ventilator. We stayed the night with Dylan and realized our little boy was in for the fight of his life.

The pressure in Dylan's head continued to rise through the night. The following morning, the doctors told us they were afraid Dylan's brain was going to swell to a point that would cut off the blood supply to his brain. Although slim, our only hope was that Dylan's brain would stop swelling before that happened. Unfortunately, each CT scan showed less and less blood flow. It was about this time we were asked if we wanted to speak to someone from a place called Gift of Hope about organ donation. I was like, *Wait... what? Donate his organs? Are you kidding me? I just want to know when he can go home!* I wanted nothing to do with it. I was partially immersed in one of the most common myths about organ donation. I couldn't help but think people were just after my son's organs!

The way I remember it, and it's possible it really didn't go down this way, but up until that time, I don't recall being told or hearing anybody tell us that Dylan was definitely going to die, had died, or was brain dead. Although that's where things were headed, which I'm sure the staff knew, no one up to that point had used those terms. I was fairly angry. In addition, organ donation was the last thing on my mind. It just isn't something you think about while you're holding hope that your seven-year-old son will somehow pull through. Time and further CT scans revealed blood flow to Dylan's brain did eventually stop. It wasn't until after this that we heard the words "brain dead." When those words were finally used, I made it clear; I needed proof, especially before agreeing to organ donation. The doctors let us watch as Dylan was injected with a contrast fluid that would show his blood flow throughout his body on a monitor. We watched as the fluid began to flow – first within his body, then his shoulders, and then his arms. We waited for it, but we never saw anything happen in his head. One last test needed to be performed before Dylan was "officially" pronounced with brain death – a physical brain death test performed by multiple doctors and nurses. We were warned no one wants to witness the final testing, so we were asked to step out. At one point during the wait, a nurse came out and said they needed us immediately. I wondered what might be going on.

Upon entering the room, to the right, I could see Dylan surrounded by about eight doctors and nurses. They had him suspended in the air by his limbs. In front of me was the head doctor. He told me that Dylan did not have a pulse, and he asked me if I wanted to remove care and pronounce him dead. What a horrible dream! Upon being asked this question, my mind went into immediate panic and analysis paralysis. I was standing there in front of the doctor, mumbling "um, uh, um, uh" over and over again. So many things were going through my mind, one of which was: no pulse meant no donation.

What seemed like an eternity of mumbling "uh" and "um" was interrupted by one of the doctors holding Dylan, announcing he had a pulse! At the same time, it was clear that Dylan didn't pass this final test. The doctor and I looked at each other for a moment, and then he looked at his watch. I looked up at the clock on the wall, and Dylan was pronounced with brain death at 12:20 pm on Friday, July 13th, 2007. Yes – Friday the 13th. Dylan passed away on a Friday the 13th, and his oldest brother was born on a Friday the 13th.

The Decision to Donate

After all we had been through since the accident and pronouncing Dylan brain dead, the ultimate decision to donate his organs was not difficult. We had talked about organ donation as a family when our son Nicholas was getting his driver's license. The actual process, however, was heart wrenchingly difficult because of what it meant. It meant Dylan was gone, and he was not coming home.

After we agreed to donate Dylan's organs, we were introduced to Melissa Williams from Gift of Hope. She was very patient with us, extremely compassionate, and answered all our questions. But most importantly, through our conversation, she completely erased my pre-conceived notion that these people were only after my son's organs. After signing all the papers, the Gift of Hope staff took over Dylan's care, and he was kept on mechanical support until the organ testing and coordinating was completed. It was Saturday afternoon, July 14th, at 4:30 pm when he finally left for the operating room to donate. 2007 was a time before donors were given the now beautiful and sacred "honor walk." Dylan's honor walk consisted of my wife Lisa, myself, Melissa, nurses from Gift of Hope, and a couple of nurses from the hospital. Upon reaching the elevator doors, we were informed that we could not go any further. As any loving mother and father would do, we tried to reassure Dylan everything would be OK. It was so hard – I was bawling my eyes out and just wanted to collapse. To this day, I do not know how I did not. Then, the miracles of life, love, and donation began. They started with Lisa receiving the glory of seeing Dylan go to heaven.

TO DYLAN, FROM MOMMY

written by Lisa Richardson

I was not asleep as some people might think. Daddy and I came home on Saturday July 14th. Uncle Scott drove us home in Daddy's car. The Star Wars toys that you received from Aunt Blair and Uncle Ryan were still in the back seat. Their wedding, which you were ring -bearer in, was just seven days ago, but it seemed like a lifetime ago.

Daddy and I fell asleep at times, holding hands, on the way home. I do not remember coming in the house. I do not remember if Nick and Bryan were home. I took a shower. The first one at home since everything happened. It felt like a long time. I got dressed and laid down on the made bed. The bedroom door was open about halfway, not closed but not fully open. I thought I would lie there for a bit and try my best to figure out what had happened to our family in the last three days and four nights since we had gone grocery shopping.

My knees were drawn up, my hair was wet, and my arms were at my side when I felt an incredible bright light come over my body –

so bright that I remember my closed eyes squinting but remaining closed at this incredible bright light. I saw an "opening" with child faces. It looked like a beautiful blue sky with clouds afloat. I saw a man. A sad figure in white was to the left. To the right of this sad figure, I saw a little blonde girl and two other dark-haired figures to the right and left of her. There was another little blonde girl to the far right. There were four angels in total to greet you. Then I saw you. I saw your full head. My view stopped at your shoulders. Your beautiful hair, as it was before it was cut. Your face… you looked scared and confused but still you rose. Your eyes were closed. Your chin raised up a bit, almost like a challenge pose. You seemed to float.

The bright lights were all around the children's faces, the sad figure, and you, Dylan. I bolted up off the bed. That is the only word to describe my action. I bolted up, arms flailing, crying. It took just a second, maybe a millisecond, to realize that you, your soul, had just arrived in heaven!

I recall being thankful and so incredibly sad. Thankful that, if you could not be with me, Daddy, Nick, and Bryan, then you were in the next best place. You were greeted. You were welcomed. You are loved. I remember my head turning and looking at Daddy's clock, which is always set ahead. I subtracted about 40 minutes and came away with what I thought was maybe 9:00, 9:15 pm.

It was not a dream, Dylan. I felt you arrive in heaven. The next morning, I received confirmation.

Dad and I had slept from pure exhaustion when we got home. I do not remember how much I slept that first evening. I heard the phone ring about 9:00 am Sunday morning. I literally stumbled from our bed to the kitchen phone. I picked it up, said hello softly, and heard a soft voice ask "Lisa?" I do not know how I answered, but I said yes. Melissa told me it was her. She was sorry if she woke me up. How silly, I remember thinking. She asked if she could talk with me for a bit. I sat down in my chair at the kitchen table and said, "Yes, of course." She proceeded to tell me that the procurement of your organs was successful. Your surgery took about four hours. Your kidneys went to a 65-year-old gentleman in Kansas. Your liver went to a 15-year-old boy in Chicago, and your heart was given to a 13-year-old girl in South Carolina. The surgery was complete at about 9:15 Saturday evening. I remember getting chills from my scalp down my entire body to my toes. My heart breaking and my breath catching, I said, "Thank you." I vaguely remember Melissa saying that if we needed anything, please call. She was incredibly sorry for us, and I knew she was crying while talking with me.

Although major organs left your body, Dylan, you were cared for and loved. I believe it takes some time before we know where we will rest. Some call it "judgment day." I believe that time caught up with me so I could be shown your fate. For that, I am so grateful, and I thank you. I have not lost you, dear Dylan. I know exactly where you are. You are safe and you are surrounded by love. You exist, you laugh, you play, you run, you swing, and you jump. You smile, you inspire, and you love. We honor, cherish, miss, and love you every single day.

Powerful stuff! I wish I was able to experience what Lisa did.

Community Love and Support

Dylan loved school, and when we lost him, despite being on summer break, the school community provided an outpouring of love and support. Lisa and I knew we wanted to do something for the school in Dylan's memory. Dylan was at his school for only two years, but the school loved him. Plus, the school has been part of my family for a long time. Not only did our two older boys, Nick and Bryan, attend that school, but I did, and all my siblings did as well. The oldest in my family attended when the school first opened in 1960. The school had a rather large courtyard area that was mostly unkempt and needed attention. I am a hobby gardener, so we thought building a garden and reading area for the children and teachers would be a wonderful way to honor Dylan and do something for the school. With the help of Dylan's first-grade teacher, we did just that. The area included a natural site for a reading spot. We paid special attention to this area and affectionately now call it "Dylan's Garden." We cleared out the area, and with the help of a professional landscaper, we started a wonderful garden. We also donated two benches, with the school's name engraved on them, for anyone to sit and read, or just to enjoy the garden.

About six weeks after Dylan's passing, we found out a little bit more about where his organs went. Dylan's kidneys went to a 65-year-old man in Kansas named Joe. Who knew that a seven-year-old's kidneys could help an older man? Dylan's liver went to a 15-year-old boy named Ali. Although his transplant took place in Chicago, Ali actually lives in the United Arab Emirates – halfway around the world! We also learned that Dylan's heart went to a 13-year-old girl in South Carolina.

Our Superhero

Dylan was now a true superhero! He helped save three lives around the world! We are happy Dylan was able to help other people. Although the people he helped are not our son, our son is now part of them. Dylan and organ donation have brought us together into an incredibly special relationship with these people that only few can comprehend, or even understand. I have written letters to the recipients, telling them about Dylan and our life since he has been gone. I shared how glad we were that Dylan was able to help them. I have sent them pictures of his elementary school's library, where they dedicated a portion in Dylan's honor, and of the memorial gardens planted both at home and at school.

We have since received letters from the kidney and liver recipients, but not yet from the heart recipient. A quote from Joe's letter, the 65-year-old man in Kansas: "Your son saved my life. My hope is that you find joy and solace in knowing he lives through me."

From the family of Ali, the 15-year-old boy in the United Arab Emirates: "Ali can now play and do everything as a normal child, and he is taking care of the precious gift you have given him. He always remembers to pray and be thankful to Dylan, the person who saved his life. Dylan is now one of our family members, and we will celebrate his birthday every year on May 11th. We pray for God to bless his soul and bless you all... Thank you."

My initial hesitation in donating Dylan's organs involved bad timing and was purely an emotional response. In the end, however, we are grateful Dylan was able to help others. We are genuinely happy for the recipients. We look forward to the day when we might even get to meet all of them in person. We have met Joe, a lifelong Shriner. He has spent his entire adult life helping children, and now a child, of all people, helped him in return. How wonderful is that? Meeting and getting to know Joe and his family has truly been a highlight in our lives! I have spoken to Ali on the phone and text him occasionally. We remain hopeful that we will one day connect with the young woman who received Dylan's heart.

I am now incredibly grateful we were asked about donation because what if... what if someone at the hospital had not asked? Dylan would have just died, nothing *more*. But now, something good has come out of such a tremendous loss. That truly gives us something to hold on to. If we were not asked, we would not have the solace and pride in knowing that Dylan saved others. I would not have these wonderful lifesaving stories to share.

Don't get me wrong, the pain from losing Dylan remains strong, and it has been a tough road. Talking about organ donation and sharing Dylan's story, although difficult, is one part of keeping Dylan alive for us. I would not want what happened to Dylan and my family to happen to anyone. But things happen, and if something were to happen, I want to make sure people know that organ, cornea, and tissue donation may be an option. It is the good that can come from such a loss.

Dylan has accomplished so much since he has been gone! He has been on posters, brochures, the newspaper, and on TV! He led the Indianapolis 500, with only eight laps to go, going 230 MPH. His superhero "Dylan Card" was taped to the car's fuselage! He has been on Joey Gase's NASCAR race car multiple times! Joey is a fellow donor family member. By sharing Dylan's story, one of the most gratifying things he has accomplished is playing a direct part in helping someone else make the decision to donate. Dylan's superhero story, his picture, and his beautiful smile helped someone make that decision. He has probably affected more people than we will ever know!

Dylan truly lives on and continues to make us immensely proud! Thank you for allowing us to share our son with you. God Bless.

About Dan

Dan and his wife, Lisa, live in Aurora, Illinois. Besides Dylan, they have two other adult children, Nick and Bryan, and one grandchild, Gracelynn.

After Dylan gave the gift of life through donation, Dan and Lisa received much solace in knowing Dylan saved others. This resulted in Dan and Lisa becoming ambassadors for the Gift of Hope Organ & Tissue Donor Network. They served on the Gift of Hope Donor Family Advisory Council for many years, and continue to advocate for organ, tissue, and eye donation. Dan also continues to keep Dylan's legacy alive by speaking at Gift of Hope sponsored events. Dan often says, "Dylan saved three lives through donation. If you could, wouldn't you too?"

In their spare time away from full-time jobs, Dan and Lisa enjoy a good bicycle ride, going for walks, traveling, gardening, and spending time with their granddaughter. Dan specifically likes gardening, woodworking, and biking. Lisa loves to read a good book and enjoys watching her favorite TV dramas.

Chill'n at home in typical male Richardson tradition, no shirt!

With his new bike!

Dylan was honored as a local HERO and honorary race starter at a NASCAR race at Chicagoland Speedway in Joliet, IL (2016). Photo Credit, Kar Silver

Dylan honored at a Kane County (IL) Cougar's Baseball Game!

Dylan with donor son, NASCAR driver, Joey Gase!

At Dylan's Great Uncle and Great Aunt's wedding. (Picture taken 4 days prior to accident)

Dylan LOVED the Outdoors!

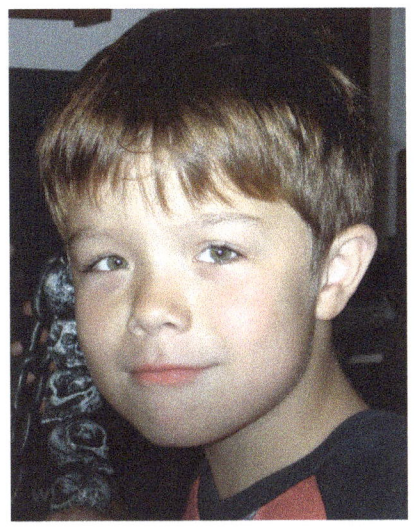

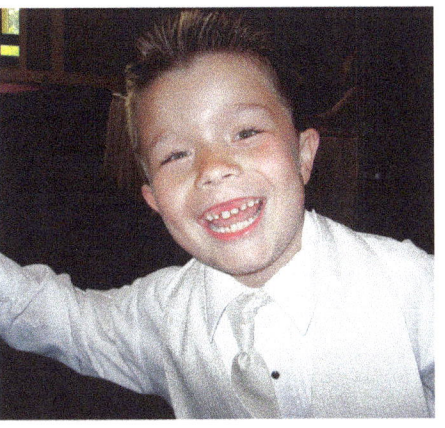

At Dylan's Great Uncle and Great Aunt's wedding. Two front teeth hanging by a thread! (Picture taken 4 days prior to accident)

Mr. Handsome!

The Family at Dylan's Great Uncle and Great Aunt's wedding.

Dylan honored with Joey Gases' Mother (Donor) on Joey's NASCAR racecar at Chicagoland Speedway with Allosource and Donate Life - 2014.

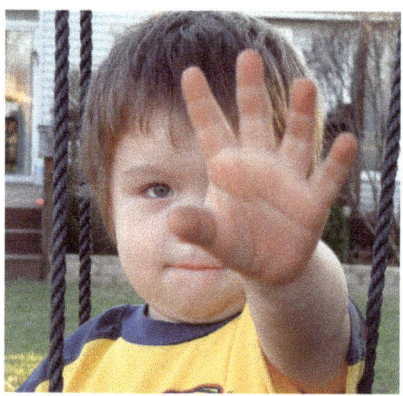

Dylan's famous "Talk to the Hand!"

The Family with Joey Gase - honored with Joey Gases' Mother (Donor) on Joey's NASCAR racecar at Chicagoland Speedway with Allosource and Donate Life - 2014.

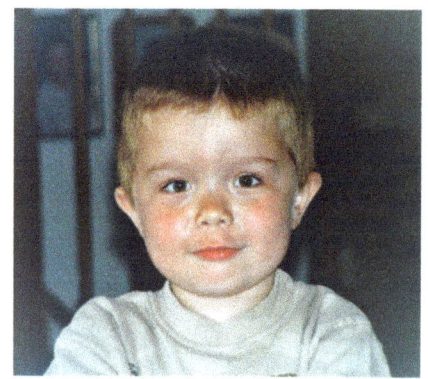

Smiling Dylan!

"I'm a SuperHero!" Spiderman (his Favorite) shirt!

Juliana's Journey

By Riki Graves

I was six-weeks pregnant when I found out I had breast cancer. My husband and I had just temporarily relocated to my hometown in Corpus Christi, Texas; he was stationed in another part of the state, working full-time for the Texas Army National Guard. I was teaching group fitness classes and looking for a job in my field, healthcare administration. I was happy to be pregnant with our second child. Our son, Ben, was two and a half at the time. He was so happy to be in Corpus near his grandparents and the beach. My husband, Chris, was home in Corpus with us three to four days a week, and then he would travel back to North Texas to work in Brownwood, a small town about an hour and a half south of Abilene.

I had taken a pregnancy test while we were in Austin on one of Chris's work trips, and we were surprised to find it positive; we'd been trying to conceive for several months. Now that I was pregnant again, I knew I would have to find a new obstetrician in Corpus. I went to a physician who was referred by a friend and highly recommended. I liked her immediately. At my first visit with her to confirm my pregnancy, I told her that I had a small lump on my breast that may need to be checked. She felt it and agreed I should go for an ultrasound "just to be sure." I really hadn't thought much about it since my family doctor in Brownwood had checked it and wasn't too concerned. Life was moving fast these days, and I just needed to confirm that it was nothing.

The next week, I went to have an ultrasound, and possibly a simple procedure if necessary. When the radiologist wasn't able to aspirate the lump, he immediately told me he would give me an anesthetic and take a biopsy. I didn't think much of it and went home to enjoy the weekend with Ben and Chris. On Sunday, Chris had to leave to go back to Brownwood. Monday was my thirty-eighth birthday. I had a nice lunch with my aunt and then went to the nail salon while Ben was at school. We were having the family over for birthday cake that evening to celebrate. While I was at the nail salon, I got a phone call from my doctor's office. It was her medical assistant telling me I needed to come to the office right away to speak with the doctor. I was concerned, but still in good spirits. I told them I would head that way as soon as I was finished at the salon. When my doctor walked into the exam room, she had tears in her eyes. She said she was so sorry to tell me the lump in my breast had come back positive for cancer. I was shocked and immediately thought, "Well, this is going to suck." She told me it was uncommon for a woman to be diagnosed with breast cancer during pregnancy and that no doctor in Corpus Christi would be able, or willing, to treat me. She immediately sent me to MD Anderson Cancer Center in Houston.

After answering some of my questions, my doctor assured me the doctors at MD Anderson treated women in my situation. They would know how to treat my breast cancer, while also caring for the growing baby inside of me. Right away, I thought I might lose the pregnancy in order to treat the breast cancer, but she was confident I could still have a healthy pregnancy. She told me I would still see her in Corpus for my prenatal care, and I would also have to start being seen at the maternal-fetal clinic since I now had a high-risk pregnancy.

I don't remember if I cried much during the visit; it seemed like my doctor was more upset than I was. I think everything hit me when I got in the car and called my husband to tell him the news.

Chris immediately broke down and started crying. He asked if he was going to lose me, and I told him I was sure I would be okay, but that we needed to start planning to get to Houston.

The next week was a blur. We made it to Houston, and MD Anderson had packed all of my appointments into several days. My new oncologist assured me I would be okay, but I would need surgery, chemotherapy, and radiation. I saw specialists in genetics, nutrition, social work, and surgery. Typically, the oncologist and surgeon would recommend a double mastectomy, but since I was pregnant, that procedure would be too invasive. The team settled on a segmental mastectomy, or lumpectomy, and hoped to get clear margins. Before I could be cleared for surgery, I had to go to Texas Children's Hospital to see their maternal-fetal medicine (MFM) physician. I felt fortunate because my oncologist and the MFM physician used to practice at the same academic hospital together, and they still had a strong relationship. The oncologist treats the mother's cancer, while the MFM physician cares for the baby during treatment. This kind of specialized care is rarely found outside of academic medicine, so I was very glad to be at the Texas Medical Center with the world's best medical teams.

Over the next few weeks, I was cleared by MFM for surgery to remove the tumor. My team agreed they would send off the sample for testing to see what type of tumor it was, how aggressive it was, and what treatment would be best for me. I was just starting my second trimester, and my oncologist thought I would probably need chemotherapy.

My results came back showing that it was an aggressive type of tumor, but we had clear margins and it was estrogen positive. That meant the tumor, or tumor cells, would keep growing while I was pregnant and producing a lot of estrogen. The plan was to have my lymph nodes removed during the segmental mastectomy, but the special dye that the surgeons use to find the lymph nodes couldn't be used because it would hurt the baby. Thus, my tumor was successfully removed, but the oncologist didn't know if I still had any cancer in my lymph nodes. Chemotherapy was recommended because of my young age and the aggressive type of cancer.

I went back to Corpus Christi to visit an oncologist that collaborated with MD Anderson, and he set me up for all of my infusion appointments, starting with port placement. He was very kind and compassionate, as well as extremely knowledgeable. I knew he would take good care of me, but I got a strange feeling when he handed me the brochure for wigs, since I would be losing my hair. My office was around the corner, and I remember going back there and sobbing because I didn't want to have chemotherapy. I felt like my mother's intuition was telling me it wasn't safe. This feeling overwhelmed me, and I immediately called my oncologist to tell him I didn't feel comfortable doing chemotherapy during the pregnancy. I asked him if he would still be my doctor even though I was going against his advice. He said he would, but he also said I would have to have another surgery to make sure I had no cancer in my lymph nodes before he could fully allow me to skip chemo. He shared that I needed to start radiation immediately after I gave birth and also go on a drug that prevents recurrence. I agreed, and my next surgery was scheduled for the next couple of weeks.

In the interim, we had our 20-week anatomy scan to see if the baby was healthy, and also to find out if we were having a boy or a girl. I knew we were having a girl because there was so much estrogen coursing through my system. Chris was home for the anatomy scan in Corpus Christi, and we were thrilled to find out that we were indeed having a baby girl. The ultrasound technician was having trouble getting some pictures of her heart, so the physician said they would refer us to a fetal cardiologist to rule out any abnormalities. We didn't think much of it and made the appointment for early the following week. Chris had to return to Brownwood, so I was on my own for the fetal cardiology appointment. It was on a Tuesday, and

I had my lymph node surgery scheduled at MD Anderson for that Friday.

Tuesday evening, I went to the fetal cardiology appointment alone. My family was taking Ben to his holiday recital at his school, and I was planning to meet them there after the appointment. During the ultrasound, the fetal cardiologist looked shocked while he was looking at pictures of my baby's heart. He asked his resident to come in and look; they were both intensely reviewing what they saw on the screen. He told me our baby girl had a condition called hypoplastic left heart syndrome (HLHS), and her heart was very malformed; only one side of her heart was growing normally. The left side was not growing and had some physical defects. I asked the doctor if he had read my chart and if he knew I also had breast cancer. He said yes and he was very sorry to tell me this news. I told him I was already seeing a doctor at Texas Children's Hospital (TCH) in Houston, and I thought I should transfer all of the pregnancy care there. I knew they would be better equipped to deal with our daughter's heart issues. He told me that if she survived the pregnancy, she would need to be at a large academic center where they offered specialized care for babies like her. I finally broke down, crying and sobbing. I texted Chris to tell him it was really bad and that I would call him when I left. The fetal cardiologist assured me he would do everything he could to get our baby's care transferred right away, and they sent me home with her scans so I could take them to TCH.

In the car, I finally called Chris. He was worried because I was so upset and could barely talk. I told him the baby's heart wasn't growing correctly and she was very sick. I also shared that the fetal cardiologist told me our baby may not survive the pregnancy. If she did, she would need heart surgery a few days after birth, then again at three months, and once more at three years. Each surgery was high risk, and the time between surgeries, when her heart would be recovering and not fully functional, would be as well. He was heartbroken and agreed we needed to have TCH take care of her. I made it to the recital for Ben, and he was standing on stage singing as I walked into the church. As soon as he was done, I rushed over and picked him up, sobbing into his little shoulder. My mom noticed and asked what was wrong. I was barely able to tell her the devastating news. We left and went home to discuss the situation. The plan was to get our baby daughter to TCH as fast as possible.

The next day, I called my team at MD Anderson and my MFM team at TCH. I needed to get an appointment at TCH with fetal cardiology the next day, because my surgery was scheduled for Friday. I spent all day on the phone with both hospitals on Wednesday. I secured an afternoon appointment with fetal cardiology at TCH on Thursday. Chris came home on Wednesday to take me to Texas Medical Center for our baby's appointments on Thursday and for my lymph node surgery on Friday.

On the drive to Houston, we chose our baby girl's name because so many people had been asking us. They wanted to pray for her by name. We chose Juliana (a name I had always loved) and Eileen, my mom's and my middle name. Juliana Eileen now had an army of people praying for her to survive and live a full life.

Fetal cardiology spent two hours with us Thursday afternoon and confirmed Juliana's diagnosis. She had HLHS with a hypoplastic (narrowed) aortic arch and a mitral valve that was not allowing blood to properly flow out of her heart. For now, my heart was beating for hers. Our fetal cardiologist told us Juliana was very sick, but assured us she had taken care of a lot of kids with her condition and she could still live a full life. TCH was the best hospital in the country for this type of heart surgery, and they had really good outcomes. She told us there was still a chance Juliana wouldn't survive the pregnancy because her heart was so sick. I shared that I was also dealing with my breast cancer diagnosis, and I needed to ask the tough questions. "What do other parents do in our situation? Do they terminate the pregnancy?" While my heart was beating for her, she was also contributing to the fact that my breast cancer was uncontrolled due to all of the estrogen in my system. I had already been told that I could not have another pregnancy because it would be too dangerous with my breast cancer history.

The cardiologist told me we had two weeks to decide what we wanted to do. There were laws in place if a pregnancy needed to be terminated. She suggested we get genetic testing done on Juliana to make sure she didn't have any other abnormalities that could make her incompatible with life. She also told me that if I had chosen to do chemotherapy, I would have gravely risked Juliana's life, which was already in a very delicate state. My surgery that Friday confirmed I did not have any cancer in my lymph nodes, and I was clear to proceed through the pregnancy without any chemotherapy.

We went home and had genetic tests done, which confirmed that Juliana did not have any conditions, besides her heart, that would affect her life. Our baby had a sick heart inside a perfect body. We chose to continue the pregnancy and pause my cancer treatment while we focused on Juliana. Every month, we had fetal cardiology appointments at Texas Children's to monitor her heart as she grew. The team asked me to "grow a big baby," so Juliana would be big enough to have heart surgery after she was born. Each fetal cardiology appointment lasted at least two hours. They took thousands of pictures and measurements of Juliana's heart as she was developing in the womb. Chris was at every appointment, and we were fortunate to have TRICARE, the military healthcare, cover all our expenses and healthcare costs.

In March, we were told Juliana's heart was getting worse and that we should pack a suitcase for our next appointment "just in case." Her due date was May 9th. At the end of March, we went to TCH for our regular fetal cardiology appointment and saw a new cardiologist that day. He was young and also had young kids at home. He told us Juliana's heart was declining and we would need to be monitored at the hospital until she was born. We were admitted to the antepartum unit at TCH's Pavilion for Women (PFW).

The hospital room was huge and only two years old. There was a comfortable bed for Chris, as well as a recliner for extra seating. I was hooked up to monitors all day that checked Juliana's heart rate and fetal activity. We settled in our room and were prepared to be there for the next six weeks. The care we received at the PFW was amazing. They had daily activities for the moms there, and I was able to meet other moms in similar situations. One mom was pregnant with conjoined twins. She went on to successfully deliver her baby girls and share their separation story on international news. It was amazing to be in a room with moms who were all going through very complicated pregnancies and still in good spirits. We knew we were in the best place for our sick babies, and we all bonded over those next few weeks.

On the morning of April 9th, Juliana's fetal activity began to rapidly decline. The goal was to let her grow big enough, but not let her get close to fetal demise before she could be delivered. The on-call MFM physician came to my room that morning and told us they were preparing to deliver Juliana in a few hours. I would have an emergency C-section, and Juliana would be taken straight to the cardiovascular intensive care unit (CVICU). They would evaluate her to get her hooked up to the necessary machines. The plan was to stabilize her and start her on medications to keep her heart beating until they had a plan.

When Juliana was delivered, there were about thirty people in the room with us. Not only was there a team to do my surgery, but there was also an entire team of neonatal intensivists ready to take care of Juliana. We were scared she wouldn't survive the birth, or her time in the CVICU. Luckily, she was born without incident, and I was able to take a peek at her and touch her before she and Chris were whisked away to the CVICU.

Since I had had an emergency C-section, we didn't have any family with us at the hospital. I was in my postpartum room all alone, with no updates from Chris, worrying about Juliana. After a bit, Chris was able to call me and tell me that she was so beautiful and was holding his hand. It's excruciating for a mother to be away from her baby, especially an extremely sick baby, so I felt like I was being tortured. I finally made it back to my postpartum room in a new unit and waited for updates from the nurses and Chris. He stayed with her all night while I waited until I was cleared to go to the West Tower (now Wallace Tower), where she was being cared for by the CVICU team.

Juliana was born at 3:30 pm, weighing 6 pounds, 14 ounces, on April 9th, 2014. I wasn't able to see her until April 10th at about noon. The wait was unlike any pain I have ever experienced. FaceTime with Chris from the CVICU didn't make the pain of a mother being away from her baby go away. When I was finally able to see her, they said that the cardiologists had been doing testing all day, and they needed to have a meeting with us to discuss a plan for her. We knew there was a possibility that she was not a candidate for surgical repair, because her most recent echocardiograms showed worsening heart function and more severe defects.

Our nurse on April 10th was named Shannon. She was in training with the charge nurse, and was very kind and empathetic. She had decorated Juliana's pod with drawings to go along with the drawing of her name that the night nurse had created. Shannon had the awful task of coming with us while we met with the surgical team to discuss Juliana's case. The chief surgeon at that time was known for having a gruff bedside manner, and he was waiting for us in the room with some other cardiologists and critical care specialists.

The chief surgeon for the entire Texas Children's Hospital system told us there was no way he could surgically repair Juliana's heart. He said it was too malformed and the actual heart muscle was very weak. He feared that if they put her on the bypass machine during surgery, her heart would not start beating again after it was repaired because it would be too weak. He told us we could take Juliana home on hospice or keep her in the hospital, hooked up to machines for as long as she could survive. It was up to us what we wanted to do. We both put our heads in our hands and sobbed because we had had so much hope for Juliana, and now he was telling us there was no hope for her. Our nurse, Shannon, gave us hugs and said she would give us some time to process everything. As the chief surgeon got up to leave the room, he said, "I mean, you could try for a heart transplant, but you'll never get a baby heart." Then he left, and I didn't see him again until a few months later.

The issue with getting a baby heart is the wait time. It is typically between three to six months, but our Juliana didn't have that long. She needed a heart right away. I wanted to give her my heart. We were devastated and called family to come as soon as possible, because we didn't know how long we had with our precious baby girl. Family arrived, and we discussed whether or not to list Juliana for a heart transplant. My dad and brother, who were both in the medical field, agreed we should at least try for a heart transplant. We wanted to give Juliana any possible chance at life – no matter how slim that chance was.

The process to be listed for a transplant is intense. Juliana had to undergo more testing to make sure she had the proper anatomy to receive a new heart and to make sure she didn't have any genetic conditions that would cause her to reject a new organ. We also had to be interviewed. We met with a social worker to discuss if we would be able to take care of her as a medically fragile child. We met with transplant cardiology to make sure we understood how important it was to come to all of her post-transplant appointments. We met with immunology, pharmacy, and a financial specialist who had to confirm that we had coverage for her post-transplant medications and medical appointments. Then we met with an infectious disease specialist. She told us Juliana would never be able to swim in a lake or river, go to Chuck E. Cheese, or be around sick people without the risk of contracting a life-threatening infectious disease. Juliana was going to be immune suppressed, and this meant we had to be extra careful with her. We also had to agree to get all of her childhood immunizations on the CDC's recommended schedule, as well as flu shots for her and the entire family every year. Anyone who wanted to be around her should also be up to date on their vaccines as well. We were overwhelmed but agreed to be good stewards of a new heart if one became available. Juliana was approved for the heart transplant waiting list at eleven days old.

During the wait, Juliana's health rapidly declined. Some of her organs were beginning to fail, and her team was very concerned that she may not be able to survive a 12-hour surgery. Her liver was also failing, and she was jaundice. She had to fight for the chance to survive and receive a perfect heart for her frail body.

On day sixteen of Juliana's life, at 4:30 am, we received a call from the CVICU. She had slightly improved the past two days and was now tolerating milrinone, a medication used to support patients in heart failure before and during cardiac surgeries. Anytime a call comes from the CVICU in the middle of the night, you always fear the worst. Chris dreaded answering the phone, but for some reason, I had a feeling it was the call we needed to proceed. It was Juliana's nurse coordinator on the phone. She said that they had accepted a heart for Juliana, and we needed to pack and get to the hospital right away. We made it to the hospital at 5:00 am on April 26th.

We filled out surgery consent forms as the team got Juliana ready for surgery. We called our families, and my mom, aunt, and Ben packed so they could be there during Juliana's 12-hour surgery. The day went by slowly as we waited for everyone to be prepped for surgery – Juliana, the surgeons, the surgical team. One of our friends in the hospital had received her gift the night before, and the surgeons were running on very little sleep, so they needed time to rest. At about 5:00 pm, the team was ready to go. The recovery surgeon met with us and introduced us to his team. He had transplanted the night before, so he was procuring the heart for Juliana tonight. We met with our transplant surgeon, who had procured the heart the night before, and he let us say our goodbyes to Juliana before she was wheeled back to the operating room to be prepped.

For some reason, I felt calm about the surgery, even though the team told us Juliana had a 50% chance of surviving it. I was confident she was in the best hospital, with the most qualified team, and had the best chance of getting a perfect heart. If she didn't survive, I knew we had done everything medically possible to save her life.

My mom, aunt, and Ben arrived by the afternoon, and we waited in the Ronald McDonald suite for updates from the operating room. The surgical nurse provided us with updates throughout. She let us know Juliana was under anesthesia and the procurement team had arrived at the donor's hospital. We were notified when the donor heart was recovered and when they began to open Juliana's chest. It's all a beautifully synchronized event on both sides, where any mishap can halt the entire process.

Late that evening, they told us the donor heart would be arriving via ambulance and to watch out the windows for an ambulance with flashing lights to pull up to the entrance of West Tower. We watched the heart arrive the entire way down Main Street, and we knew that Juliana was about to receive the most precious gift in the entire world. "The donor heart has arrived!" was the next text we received. They would let us know when the team was ready to implant it into Juliana's chest, and again when it was beating. At 1:08 am on April 27th, 2014, Juliana's donor heart began beating in her tiny chest. I instantly felt at peace. The surgeon later told us it began beating right away.

Chris and I decided to get some sleep in the recliners at the Ronald McDonald House, while they finished up in the operating room. We knew our surgeon would come give us an update, but we had been up for almost twenty-four hours and were exhausted from lack of sleep and the emotional rollercoaster. My mom and aunt took Ben back to our apartment; so they could all get some rest as well. About 4:30 am, the surgeon came out to give us an update.

He woke up Chris, but they forgot to wake me up! He told him the surgery went beautifully, and Juliana was headed to a private room in the CVICU. I woke up and needed to pump milk for Juliana, and afterwards I snuck upstairs to the CVICU so I could put it in the refrigerator for her. I ran into one of her nurses and asked if I could peek in to see her. She took me over to her and said, "Can you believe it? She's pink!" She looked like a different baby now that her skin was pink instead of a pale grey. I wasn't prepared, however, for how swollen she was, and that one side of her face was twice the size of the other side. Our surgeon stopped by to check on her and told me he was very happy with her surgery and her new heart. It was a miracle that our baby finally had a chance at life.

Over the next few days, we sat by her bedside all day long and went to our apartment to rest at night. One evening, three days later, we received a call from her bedside nurse that Juliana had just spiked a fever, and she had called the cardiologist to check on her. We received updates throughout the night and found out the next morning she was in septic shock. Her doctors told us she was as sick as she was before her transplant, and they were not sure she could survive this infection. Four machines were continuously running to pull fluid off of her tiny body from lines in her chest and abdomen. The team didn't know the cause, but they knew she had to fight again for her life. Thankfully, after about a week of fighting, Juliana turned the corner and stabilized again. We were hopeful and ecstatic.

The next couple of weeks in the CVICU went by quickly. I started my radiation and would walk across the street from Texas Children's to go to the Mays Clinic at MD Anderson each day. My radiology technicians were fascinated by Juliana's story and asked for updates. Chris and I were able to hold Juliana for the first time on Mother's Day in the CVICU. We had a wonderful nursing team that day. They grabbed some pillows and all of her lines, got her situated and put her in my arms. It was amazing for both of us to finally be able to hold our little miracle girl.

Once Juliana was extubated, we were moved down to the cardiac floor for her to continue her breathing treatments, physical therapy, and occupational therapy. Since she was born, she had been bedridden with her arms tied down, so that she wouldn't grab any of her lines. It was time for her to learn how to take a bottle and move her arms. Juliana progressed rapidly on the floor, and before we knew it, we were being discharged. We brought our daughter home on June 16th, 2014, just seven weeks after her heart transplant. She was fortunate she didn't need any breathing support, and she only needed a tiny tube in her nose for feeding and meds.

I spent my time that summer taking Juliana to weekly appointments for therapy and cardiology and going to my radiation appointments. We made our move to Houston permanent and found a house in Missouri City that was close to the medical center. Juliana continued to grow and get stronger. She loved being around her big brother Ben, who was now three, and loved to make her giggle. I spent a year taking her to TCH for medical and therapy appointments. She took her first steps with our amazing TCH physical therapist, Heather.

For Juliana's first birthday, we hosted a big party at our house with family, friends, and her nurses and therapists. It was a beautiful celebration of everyone's prayers, strength, and the medical team that had brought her through one of the most medically complex situations an infant can face.

Juliana is now eight years old and living a full life as a second grader. This year, she was chosen to be the local hero of the year for Texas Children's Hospital. She has been making the rounds at several fundraising events, helping raise money for the hospital that saved her life. Juliana wants to make sure other kids can be saved like she was. She loves playing with her friends, going to the beach, and swimming at our neighborhood pool.

I have decided to use this beautiful story to help others. I began working with some public health organizations when Juliana was two to spread awareness and promote legislation that would protect vulnerable kids like her. We have shared her story on local, national, and international platforms to promote the work Texas Children's does to care for kids who may not have a chance at another hospital, and to reiterate the importance of organ donation.

We met Juliana's donor family in 2020, when Juliana had just turned six. Since then, we have become close with them and have had several visits. Most recently, we went to her donor's big sister's quinceanera in Mississippi. Juliana participated in the event as the little sister and said it was the best day of her life. She is forever grateful to her donor, baby Christopher, who gave her life because of organ donation. His picture hangs in her room, and not a day goes by that we aren't thankful to him and his family for choosing to give the gift of life.

About Riki

Riki Graves has spent several years as a public advocate for her daughter, Juliana, who received a heart transplant at just seventeen days old. While Riki was pregnant with Juliana, she was diagnosed with breast cancer. Since surviving both difficult health challenges in 2014, Riki has been an advocate for children like her daughter, who aren't always able to advocate for themselves.

Shortly after Juliana was born, Riki began volunteering at Texas Children's Hospital with the fetal center and heart center. Through connections with Juliana's medical team, Riki became an active vaccine advocate, working with The Immunization Partnership, Immunize Texas (now HAVEN), Voices for Vaccines, and Trust for America's Health. Riki's vaccine advocacy has included being invited to testify at both the Texas Senate and the Texas House of Representatives during the past three legislative sessions. She has also worked with media on public health and vaccine advocacy pieces, as well as presented to staffers on the importance of strong vaccination policy at Capitol Hill in Washington, D.C.

Riki serves as a board member for Transplant Families and HAVEN. She is also active on ACTION Learning Network's FACT and CNOC Committees, the Pediatric Heart Transplant Society's Quality Initiatives Committee, and the American Liver Foundation's Texas Medical Advisory Committee. Riki has a master's in healthcare administration, and she is employed by Houston Methodist's J.C. Walter Jr. Transplant Center as a Business Development Specialist for the Sherrie and Alan Conover Center for Liver Disease and Transplantation.

Riki is married to Chris, a retired U.S. Army Major, and they have two children: Benjamin (12) and Juliana (9), as well as Chris's older daughters, Ebony and Olivia. The family stays active and enjoys regular trips to the beach in Corpus Christi, as well as ski trips to Colorado. Riki can be reached via email at rikigraves@gmail.com.

Riki and Juliana at a CMN event for TCH.

The Graves Family

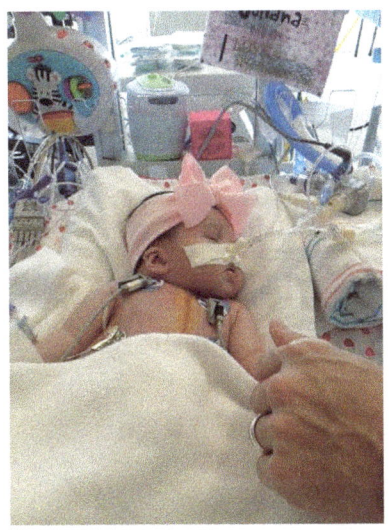

First days post-transplant.

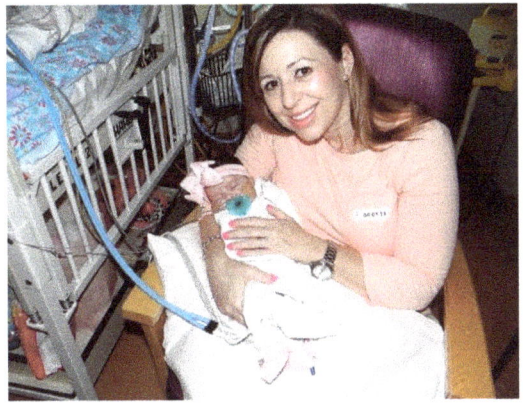

Holding Juliana in the CVICU.

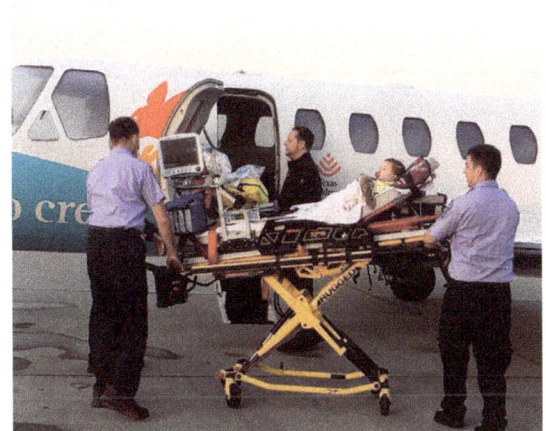

Flying back to TCH from Corpus Christi after contracting an infectious disease.

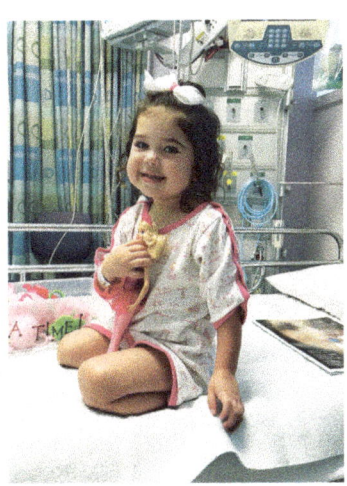

Heart biopsy day at TCH.

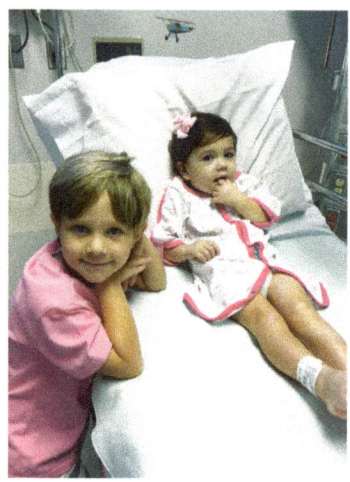

*Ben cheering up Juliana
in the hospital.*

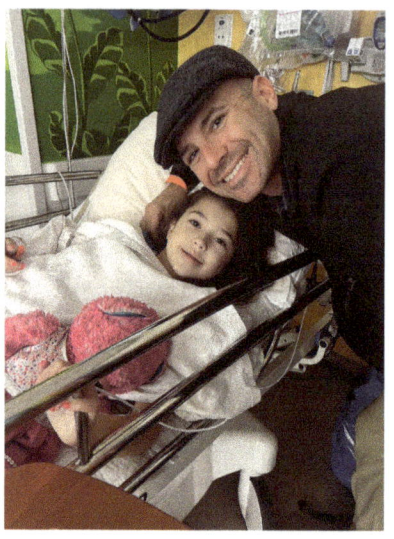

*Chris and Juliana at TCH
for her 2022 biopsy.*

Celebrating Juliana's 8th birthday.

*Riki's mom helping with Juliana
during one of her TCH stays.*

Visiting Colorado at Christmas.   *Climbing trees in Corpus Christi.*

Juliana excited to be the 2022 Texas Children's Local
Hero of the Year for Children's Miracle Network.

First day back at school after COVID virtual school.

Riki and Juliana's bond, taken in Corpus Christi.

Ethan's Story

By Gail Burant

Transplant. A word that changed my life in an instant one ordinary day in August of 2009. I still remember that day like it was yesterday. My son, Ethan, was three months old and had been to the doctor for an ear infection. She felt he looked a bit jaundiced, so she decided to run a few extra tests. Ethan had his blood drawn for the first time, which was not easy to watch as a parent, especially one with a baby because their veins are so tiny. Afterwards, our doctor scheduled an ultrasound at the local hospital. Both my husband, Steve, and I went to this appointment, unaware of what to expect or the outcome that would follow. The ultrasound appointment seemed to take forever, but luckily, Ethan was his normal, happy-go-lucky self. I was a basket of nerves since I didn't even know what they were looking for, and it appeared that the tech was really searching for something. We left the hospital separately; Steve returned to work, and I headed home with Ethan. On the ride home, the doctor called. It wasn't a nurse or another healthcare person; it was our *doctor* calling. I knew this meant the situation was more than serious. She began to talk, and all I remember is me asking, "Should I pull over?" and her replying, "Yes."

I will never forget pulling into the Shopko parking lot, not really hearing all of the words she was saying until she said, "Ethan will need a liver transplant to survive." Our doctor believed Ethan had something called biliary atresia (BA), which is a rare disease that affects the bile ducts of the liver. I didn't comprehend at that moment what all of that meant, but the words "to survive" hit me hard in the gut. I honestly heard nothing else the doctor said. After hanging up, I bawled my eyes out right there in the parking lot while Ethan was peacefully asleep in his car seat. After a few minutes, I pulled it together enough to drive home and call my husband. I asked him to come home so we could talk about the news we had just received. Our family and our priest gathered that night in prayer. The next day we headed off to Children's Hospital in Milwaukee for Ethan's first of many surgeries. My mom, Grandma Linda, came to help take care of Connor, our oldest son, who was three at the time. We didn't know what to expect or just how long we would be gone.

After the couple of hours ride down from the Green Bay area, we arrived at Children's in Milwaukee. Ethan was examined, and the medical team decided he would first have a surgery to determine if his bile ducts were open or closed. Unfortunately, that surgery showed his ducts were not working like they were supposed to. Two days later, Ethan went in for a second surgery, called the *Kasai* procedure, where they tried to reroute parts of the ducts within his liver to help the bile flow. These surgeries were beyond tough, and not knowing anything about BA, or how long we would be in Milwaukee, made it even more challenging. It was also hard leaving our other son and being so far from home. However, we knew in our hearts that we were right where we needed to be to give Ethan the best chance at improving his liver function and at extending his life. It didn't take long for the doctors to tell us that the surgery we had hoped would solve the problem was not successful, and that Ethan would indeed need a liver transplant to survive.

In November, we learned that our insurance wouldn't financially cover the transplant in Milwaukee, so we had to move to a new facility. Our options for a new transplant center were farther away and located all around the country. The closest option we were given was Children's Memorial Hospital in Chicago (which is now Lurie Children's Hospital of Chicago). We chose to go there since they were the closest. We met with our new medical team, and Ethan was placed on the transplant list. We learned that another option was for Ethan to potentially receive a liver from a living donor. We didn't even know that was possible! With a living donor, only a portion of their liver is taken, and within six months, their liver regenerates itself... Wow! The human body is an amazing vessel. This meant that Steve or I could be his living donor, if one of us was a match, and we could be the key to Ethan's survival. They ruled me out because I was not Ethan's blood type, but Steve was, so he began the testing process to see if he was a match. Unfortunately, due to a variety of circumstances, Steve was not an eligible candidate to be a living donor for Ethan. We put our faith into praying for a deceased donor; all we could do at that point was pray.

During our Christmas gathering that year, our nephew, Adam, approached us about being Ethan's living donor. We were shocked, and at first, very uncomfortable with it. Adam was a member of our family, so we felt we couldn't ask someone in our family to put themselves at risk to help Ethan. To have another child (Adam was twenty-one at the time, but we still considered him a child) from our family in surgery at the same time as Ethan was too overwhelming to think about. We talked with Adam extensively, as well as with his parents, about his offer to be the living donor. This was not a decision we wanted him to make without really knowing all that was involved. Adam was still adamant about getting tested. He told us he had done the research on being a living donor, so he knew what he was offering, and he was prepared to go in and get tested. After Christmas, Adam went to Chicago to start the extensive process to see if he was a match for Ethan.

In January of 2010, shortly after Adam's testing, we learned he was indeed a MATCH! We were beyond grateful to Adam, but we were still holding out hope for a deceased donor since we still had our worries about both boys going through this process. The transplant was scheduled for early March, but God had other plans. The night before surgery, while we were all in the hospital, Ethan spiked a fever and the team determined that it was not safe to proceed with the transplant. We felt defeated but kept our faith, believing that God had a bigger plan, and that we just couldn't see it then. The transplant was rescheduled for late April.

April 26th, 2010 was a beautiful day. I remember the sun was shining bright that day in Chicago. Adam was at Northwestern Memorial in Downtown Chicago, while Ethan was at Children's Memorial, located near Lincoln Park. In my journal, I wrote, "It's a beautiful day for a transplant," and it truly was. The day was long, but by the end of the day, Ethan and Adam were out of surgery, and the transplant was a success. Praise God! The boys were each recovering in their respective hospitals. We now call Adam our "angel on Earth," and we cannot say thank you enough. Adam saved our son's life, and we are forever grateful to him for making the choice to be a living organ donor.

The first few years post-transplant were a roller coaster of illnesses, hospitalizations, road trips, and ambulance rides to Chicago for checkups and treatments. At the same time, Ethan was starting to grow and thrive as a baby boy with his new, functioning liver. We were so thankful for every milestone: the first time he rolled over, his first words, the first time he crawled, and eventually his first steps. His happy-go-lucky, laid-back personality was a godsend through this rollercoaster of a time. As his mom, I lived and breathed the Serenity Prayer, trying my best to stay focused on the positive and to not let the things that were out of my control bring me down.

Ethan went to daycare, since both Steve and I had to work to support all of the financial burdens that came along with having a chronically ill transplant child. At times, this part of the transplant world was overwhelming as a parent. But one look at our smiling toddler with his fun personality, and the worries would fade away. Looking at Ethan reminded us to be thankful for every day, every moment, and every minute that we didn't have to be in a hospital or a clinic. We lived in a world where we penciled things into the calendar, not sure of what the next day, week, or month would bring. We managed to find joy in the life we were living and to not sweat the small stuff or take anything for granted. Our family had been given a very special gift, and we didn't want to ever forget that or take it for granted.

During the first three years of Ethan's life, I had many conversations with a lot of different people about organ donation. Throughout these conversations, I realized organ donation is a topic that people don't really want to talk about. In fact, most people don't even think about it. I understood because we had never thought about it ourselves, that is until it was a part of our lives. We had never even heard of living organ donation either, especially when it came to a baby who needed a transplant. During these conversations, I learned how much the topic of organ donation needs to be talked about. It's a topic that shouldn't be avoided, yet it is uncomfortable for so many to talk about. It made me wonder what we could do, based on our experience, to help bring about that conversation.

All of these conversations, or lack thereof, gave me an idea, so I approached the other student council advisor at the school where I work. She also had a personal connection to organ donation, because she had lost her brother at a young age and he was an organ donor. We discussed different ways we could bring awareness about organ donation and how great the need is. We wanted to do something fun to raise funds, and we came up with the idea of having a fun run/ walk. It made sense to work in partnership with the students on our middle school student council, and we decided the main purpose of the walk would be to raise money for the organization Donate Life Wisconsin.

We held our first walk in April of 2013 and named it the NEW Donate Life Walk (for Northeast Wisconsin). We chose that month because April is National Donate Life month. In addition to the walk, we hosted a silent auction and raised around $4,000. Our student council members helped by asking local businesses for sponsorships, securing silent auction donations, and hanging posters to advertise the walk. We also asked various other student groups at our school as well as staff members and family and friends to help out by donating items. We even had some Green Bay Packers players attend our first walk in support of growing awareness for organ donation. I am proud to say that we just held our tenth annual walk in 2022. Through the years, we have added many facets to the walk, but my favorite part is the Gift of Life Garden Walk. This is a garden-themed trail that showcases stories from families touched by organ donation. The Garden Walk shares stories from both organ donor recipients and donor families whose loved ones live on through the gift of life because of organ donation and transplantation. This is our way of putting faces to the stories. By directly sharing the stories of affected families, we can show others just how powerful giving the gift of life can be!

We have learned that getting a transplant doesn't mean your medical journey is done. There are many hurdles and challenges that Ethan has had to face. As his mom, the transplant journey for me comes with its own challenges and tribulations. My worrying didn't end just because he had received the gift of life. I still worry about how medications might affect him and how he is handling everything mentally as he grows up and becomes more involved in his medical decision making. I also worry about how our health insurance will help or hinder his path and our family's future.

Ethan continues to battle and has on-going medical issues. In January of 2020, he went in for a regular eye exam at our local Target Optical. After a short exam, the doctor came out to share with me that he thought Ethan had a brain tumor and should be rushed to

Children's Milwaukee. My heart sank; I truly did not know how to process what I had just been told but got in the car and quickly drove to Milwaukee. Once at Children's, Ethan underwent many scans, lumbar punctures, tests, and procedures, and they determined that he had a pseudo tumor, along with idiopathic intracranial hypertension. This meant that there was an extreme amount of pressure on his optic nerve that was causing him to lose his peripheral vision. The crazy part about this "blip" in his medical journey is that Ethan had had no signs of these newfound conditions. He wasn't having headaches or seeing double, nor was he seeing black spots or feeling dizzy. He had zero symptoms, which made understanding what was happening even harder to grasp. Ethan spent about a week and a half in the hospital and was then assigned various eye specialists to follow his case. To try and help narrow down the reason for these new issues appearing post-transplant, he has had more tests, eye pictures, lumbar punctures, and scans in the last two years (2020–2022) than I can keep track of. The medical team recommended we start genetic counseling since there were markers that made the doctors believe Ethan had *Alagille syndrome*, a rare genetic disorder that can affect multiple organs, and not the biliary atresia that he was diagnosed with as a baby. Our medical team told us that less was known about Alagille syndrome thirteen years ago. The complexity and the symptoms can vary greatly from person to person, even within the same family, which is one reason why we hadn't been directed down this path sooner in our journey; Alagille syndrome wasn't on the radar of our medical team. We are currently going through more extensive genetic testing, and it has been determined that Ethan does have a variant of Alagille's. This new finding has increased the number of specialists Ethan has to see, along with our number of visits to Milwaukee.

Not every day is easy for Ethan. Being a teenager these days is tough enough, let alone adding in ten-plus different specialists to talk with and share his medical journey. Sometimes we have to make weekly trips down to Milwaukee, which means missing out on school, time with friends, time spent doing his hobbies, and time spent at home playing with our dog, Stella. We are lucky to have a wonderful support system that surrounds Ethan and our family to help us get through the tough stuff. Ethan's positive, let things roll-off-his-back attitude has also helped him take everything in stride. He has the ability to persevere through adversity and is a force to be reckoned with, one that most adults cannot match.

In August of 2022, Ethan had the amazing opportunity to attend his first ever Transplant Games of America, which are recreational competitions that take place every two years in a different city. Thousands of people gather together for the world's largest celebration of life! The 2022 Games were held in San Diego, California. It was not only Ethan's first trip to the Games, but also his first trip to California and to the Pacific Ocean. Ethan chose to participate in three events: cornhole, table tennis, and golf doubles. His golf partner was a fellow transplant recipient from Green Bay that Ethan had met through the NEW Donate Life Walk. Ethan was very nervous at his first event, table tennis, but once the matches were done, he was smiling from ear to ear, walking away with a GOLD medal! He also won gold medals in the cornhole competition and in golf doubles!! Ethan's favorite memory from the 2022 games was golfing with his partner, Darin, at Miramar Memorial Golf Course, which is located on a military base. My favorite memory was watching Ethan get out on the dance floor with his new transplant "family" aboard the USS Midway at the Quarter Century Club Dinner, which celebrates recipients and donors at their twenty-five-year mark and beyond. Attending the games was a wonderful experience. Ethan was able to just be himself around others who were just like him. This event allowed him to come out of his shell and see that he is not EVER alone in this journey. Team Wisconsin welcomed him (and me) with open arms. We made so many new, life-long friendships and cannot wait to attend the next games as a whole family!

Ethan is an energetic, fun-loving, witty, and kind-hearted thirteen-year-old. He has had to battle a multitude of medical issues in a short amount of time, but through all of these ups and downs, Ethan continues to be a ROCK STAR at life. He enjoys playing soccer at school, hanging out with his brother, and spending time helping out at Grandma and Grandpa's farm. Ethan is also involved with the choir at his school and is a member of the stage crew for his school's musical. He also enjoys playing board games with our family, and like most teenagers, he *loves* playing video games. Hockey for fun on the homemade ice rink in the backyard is another favorite pastime. Ethan is currently awaiting a Make-A-Wish grant to get an even bigger hockey rink in the backyard, one that he can use all year round, and we could not be more excited and grateful for this very special gift! We are so proud of our son, and we continue to praise God every day for the gift of life that was given to him by his angel on Earth, Adam. Ethan has taught us so much in these past thirteen years, life lessons that we never would have experienced without his illness.

It is an on-going journey, or rather the rollercoaster of life, that has taught us as a family what *true* faith is as well as what it means to have an amazing support system surrounding you no matter what. We make an effort to be grateful for every day and to not take any moment for granted, and we have learned to never sweat the small stuff!

About Gail

Secondary only to being a dedicated wife and mother, Gail is a tireless advocate for increasing awareness of the need for donors in Wisconsin. Her passion stems from her own son's story of organ transplantation. In 2013, Gail, along with her co-founder and best friend, started the NEW Donate Life Walk and silent auction. Through the walk, they have not only raised thousands of dollars over the last decade for Donate Life Wisconsin, but they have also helped educate hundreds of attendees on the need for more donors. In 2022, Gail and Ethan attended the Transplant Games of America in San Diego, CA. Here, her passion deepened, and she developed a newfound fervor for advocacy.

Gail is a recipient of the Bellin Hospital Lifesaver Wellbeing Award for her advocacy work around organ donation. She also received the Student Council Advisor of the Year for Region III from the Wisconsin Association of School Councils, in part for founding the NEW Donate Life Walk.

Gail is a French teacher at a middle school in Green Bay, Wisconsin, where she is the advisor for the French Club, as well as a former Student Council advisor. Biennially, she travels to France with high school students to immerse them in French culture. In her free time, Gail likes to scrapbook, travel, play board games, and relax by watching Hallmark movies. She also likes spending time with family on her parent's farm in Central Wisconsin. She lives in Pulaski, Wisconsin, with her husband, Steve, and their sons, Connor and Ethan.

You can connect with Gail through the NEW Donate Life Walk website: http://newdonatelifewalk.weebly.com/ or email newdonatelife@gmail.com

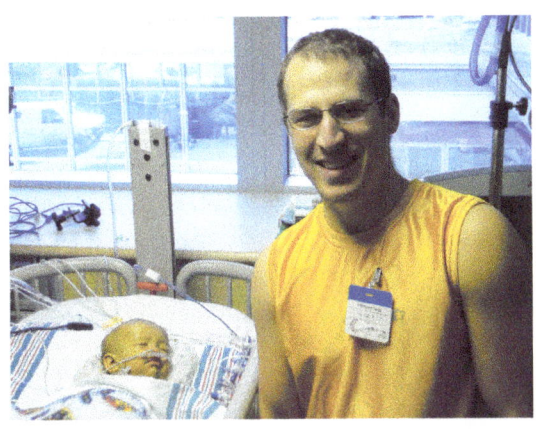

Ethan and his donor, Adam, two days post-transplant.

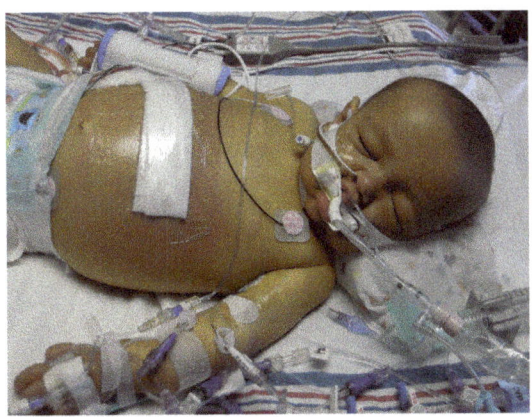

Ethan two days post-transplant.

Ethan's pre-school graduation.

Ethan and Connor at the 2014 Donate Life Walk.

Family hike.

Ethan loving life.

Ethan and his dog, Stella.

*Celebrating Ethan's five-year
liver anniversary at Disney.*

*Transplant Games, 2022,
Ethan's first gold medal in table tennis.*

*Transplant Games, 2022,
Miramar Golf gold medal.*

Ethan thanking his donor, Adam.

Visiting Lambeau Field.

Ethan on his 10-year liver birthday trip, on the Kansas City Chiefs stadium tour.

Ethan and donor, Adam.

This is the Moment You Were Created For

By Harmony Wells

"We all have special gifts to help people,
and one day you will do great things."

Our family moved to Winslow, Arizona, from Phoenix ten years ago when our oldest daughter was being severely bullied. A friend of mine had moved there, and she suggested we move there for the smaller school setting. The small town, slower pace of life, and cooler weather also sounded appealing. We fell in love with Winslow and the people we had met when we visited, so I just knew that was where we needed to live. Of course, moving north and leaving 120 plus degree weather was another great reason. Who would have ever imagined that moving to this small town would later lead to me saving a child's life.

Once in Winslow, we settled right into the community, finding jobs and getting the kiddos into schools. The school district was just what our family needed. They helped prevent my children from being bullied, and they placed my younger children into special needs programs to get them the help they needed right away. We really enjoyed life and the people in Winslow. Our kids' favorite part of town was Clear Creek. We would go there all the time just to splash around and search for tadpoles.

Growing up, my grandmother always told me, "Still hands are for the devil's work," so naturally, I have always kept myself busy. When we lived in Phoenix, I was always busy running my own small businesses in daycare and cake decorating. Now, I make soaps, lotions, custom cups, and epoxy art with my current business, KittyLux Creations. Being an entrepreneur has given me the chance to branch out into the community and meet new people. Plus, I have been able to donate to many causes and bring so many smiles to people's faces!

Despite being busy with working and taking care of my family, I fell into a funk about what I was doing in this small town. I didn't feel like I had a purpose. I longed to move back to Phoenix, but then the reminder of the heat changed my mind fast enough. I still felt I needed a change and wanted to move back to Washington State, where I had lived for several years before. My husband has always supported me in all my endeavors, so he agreed to move the family to Spokane, Washington, where we also had family. We were actively planning the move and applying for jobs when COVID-19 hit, and the state of the nation changed. I told myself there was more for me to do in Winslow and the time was not right to move.

While we were all navigating through our changing world in 2020, I heard a story about a sick little boy named Tristan. Many people in town were wearing these green bracelets that read *Tristan Strong*. Tristan also lived in Winslow and was suffering from midaortic syndrome. A friend shared his story on Facebook, and what I read just broke my soul. It's every parent's worst nightmare to receive the diagnose of "failure to thrive." Tristan was eleven years old and just one day younger than my son. I read that he had been suffering with a long history of medical problems since he was seventeen months old. He was misdiagnosed with Wilms tumor when it was actually blood clots that were causing his blood pressure to get so high that the blood vessels in his kidneys burst. He had been bleeding internally and spent more than a hundred days of his second year of life in the hospital. When Tristan turned four, they had to travel over two thousand miles to Boston to meet with a specialty team who were doing research on a disease that Tristan's symptoms seemed to reflect. During this research, he was finally diagnosed with midaortic syndrome in 2015, which is a disease that affects the heart's largest blood vessel, ultimately causing poor kidney function.

The special team also found that Tristan's kidneys were severely underdeveloped, and because of all the issues he had, they removed one of them. Tristan continued to be hospitalized every year due to complications from his kidney disease, and in April of 2020, he had to have his other kidney removed and was placed on daily overnight dialysis. In November of 2020, Tristan experienced a traumatic event right before his appointment to see the transplant team to begin the evaluation process. His body had a sudden spike in blood pressure. This caused a fluid shift in his brain, which caused seizures, headaches, lost consciousness, and airway blockage. Tristan woke up in the ICU both blind and non-verbal. It took over a month of rehabilitation for him to get well enough to be placed on the transplant list. In March of 2021, he was finally put on the transplant waiting list to receive a kidney.

I continued to follow his heartbreaking story on Facebook and prayed a lot for him and his family. Seeing that he could not attend school, go camping, jump on a trampoline, play his favorite sport, baseball, or really do most things that any eleven-year-old child wants to do was so hard to swallow. Tristan was struggling both physically and mentally and just wanted to sleep all day, even though it never felt like he could get enough rest. It was difficult for his family to plan anything, or be far from home, as he had to do dialysis each night while he slept. A good friend of mine, Mica, worked at his school, and I told her that when the time came, I would be the one to donate to him. I just had this feeling that I would be the one. I told several people my plans, and some were very excited, while others thought I was crazy. What mattered most was my husband was very supportive of my decision, and he told me if I felt that strongly about it, then I needed to do it. He would be there for me 100% of the way. I was in shock, however, at how many people were not supportive of my decision, including some of my own family. I think they were more concerned with my long-term health.

Five years ago, I underwent five esophageal surgeries. The first one was to repair an esophageal hernia that I was born with. During the surgery, they found a tumor that was taking over my stomach and esophagus. My doctor was amazing. He didn't proceed right away once they found the tumor; instead, he let me wake up to let us know the original plans had drastically changed, and even after all the imaging and testing I had had, the tumor had not shown up once. After they went back in the same day and removed the tumor, they sent it in for testing. I had to have another surgery the next day because my stomach was leaking where they had removed the tumor, since the area was so thin. My test results came back with the best news ever; the tumor was not cancerous!

I ended up having several complications, however, from those surgeries and lots of scar tissue. I was on a liquid diet and had a feeding tube most of the year. Due to scarring, my esophagus was the size of a coffee stir stick. I was even choking on my own spit. They had to do another surgery to place a mesh stent in my esophagus to prevent it from closing. I threw up several times a day because my body was trying to reject the stent. I had another surgery to remove the stent, but I continued having issues with my esophagus trying to close due to the scar tissue. My doctor had a team of doctors treating me, and over the next year, they were able to do dilation after dilation to keep my esophagus open. I am grateful for what they did for me because it saved me from getting an esophagectomy. Everyone on my team said I was too young and they were going to do everything possible to prevent me from needing an esophagectomy. It took a year, but I had a normal-sized esophagus and was able to eat most things again. I still go in once a year for dilation, but I feel great. During this ordeal, I felt like I was dying and wanted to give up several times. It was a rough thing to endure while still trying to take care of a family.

My family and friends had seen me suffer, so I could understand their hesitation and why they thought I was crazy to even think about giving up one of my kidneys for someone else. I told them, How can I not? I am happy and blessed to be healthy. I didn't have cancer, so how could I not donate to this child in need. I knew what it was like to go through medical issues, and I could only image the heartache for Tristan and his family. I knew in my heart I was his match and it was something I must do. It was my calling; I was being led to do it. This boy needed his childhood back, and I could help him. If it was my son, I would want someone to jump through fire for him as well.

I did not know Tristan's family personally, but I followed his story and eagerly waited for the post announcing they were looking for people to test to see if they were a match. I never had any doubt that my purpose in life was to save this little boy. I kept dreaming of the phone call that I would later receive from the transplant team saying I was a perfect match. Every day, I would hear the words in my head, "This is the moment you were created for." I never once wavered from my decision to get tested when the time came. When the community of Winslow needs to come together for something or someone, they do it in an abundant and amazing way. Just like the day when Tristan and his family left to drive down to Phoenix to have his last kidney removed in April of 2020. Everyone came together and honked their car horns for Tristan. I had to work so I could not participate, but my heart and prayers were with him. I could hear the honks from inside work, so I took time to pray for him and his family. I felt peace knowing he was going to be ok and that we would soon start our journey so I could share my spare with him.

In January of 2021, the Facebook post that I had been patiently waiting for finally appeared. They were looking for donors with type O blood. It was GO TIME for me! I called St. Joseph's Hospital and spoke with the transplant coordinator, Lorrie, who got all the paperwork started. Everything would be covered under the recipient's insurance. Since we lived in a smaller town, it wasn't as easy to get the bloodwork done, like it would be if we lived in a big city and could just go to a participating lab. The hospital sent me my orders and the kit that needed to be taken to a lab. I needed to have tubes of blood drawn and then overnight it back to them. Finding a lab that could help me proved to be quite difficult, and the participating lab was over three hours away. I could have done it at my local provider, but we did not have a shipping service in our small town to send it out overnight. I drove an hour away to Flagstaff and went to three different labs with no luck. They said they could do the blood draw, but I would have to pay for it, which I was okay with. The problem was they would not give me the blood samples, even though it was my blood. I was in shock that no one would help me and that this simple task had become so difficult.

When I was just about ready to give up and drive to Phoenix to get it done, I tried one more lab and pleaded with them. I told them they would be helping save a little boy's life! Finally, someone wanted to help, and the lab proceeded to process my orders. They sealed all the samples for me, and I packed it all in the shipping packaging that was provided to me by the hospital in Phoenix. Just in the nick of time, I made it to FedEx within minutes of their last truck leaving for the day. The agent smiled and said he would make sure the lifesaving package got on the truck right away. Even with those obstacles, I never doubted God's plan.

At the end of March of 2021, I received *the call*. It was the call I had been dreaming about. My transplant coordinator let me know that a few other potential donors had tested, but I was the PERFECT MATCH! I remember that day just like it was yesterday; I fell to the ground, crying tears of pure joy as I heard in my head, "This is the moment you were created for." I can't say I have ever felt like that in my life.

That was the start of trips back and forth to the hospital in Phoenix for the myriad of tests to be Tristan's donor. Even though I had been told what I already knew in my heart, I still had to go through the long process of tests and scans to ensure I was the perfect match and physically able to donate. They look for every reason why you should not donate, which is ultimately in the best interest of the donor. I had to have several extensive tests done to confirm that I did not have cancer or any underlying medical issues. On my first trip to the hospital lab, they took over twenty-three vials of blood. They also had to review my medical records. A support person was required to go with me to most of my appointments. My husband had a job, and we had three kids at home, so it wasn't really possible for him to come with me. We lived far from family and did not want to take the kids out of school just so my support person could be there.

Luckily, my dear friend, Kristel, and her husband, Chuck, lived in the Phoenix area. I let her know my exciting plans, and that I needed a place to stay after surgery since I would not be able to return home right away. The medical team wanted me to stay in Phoenix for three-plus weeks after the transplant to recover before I could make the long trip home. My friends were more than willing to support me through this journey and let me stay with them. Kristel even volunteered to be my support person and went with me to 90% of my appointments. I am forever grateful to my soul-sister for helping me through this journey and to her husband for cooking amazing food while I was there. It really felt like I was at home! Donating would have not been possible if I didn't have them! After all my trips down to Phoenix from March through May, and then after having my case go before a board of transplant professionals, I got the call that I was APPROVED to donate.

Even though I was approved, they let me know they had found something in my testing that I needed to be aware of. I had a spleen aortic aneurysm, which is an aneurysm on my spleen, but it was very small and too small for treatment. They advised me to have it monitored annually until it was big enough for treatment, but everyone agreed it was not a reason to stop the donation process. Discovering the aneurysm meant that Tristan was saving my life just as much as I was saving his!

In the middle of May, I shared the news with both of our families that I was Tristan's match. I asked Tristan to be my "bean buddy" for life. I had some fun "bean buddy" shirts made for Tristan and me. Tristan's transplant team called his mom a few days later to let her know that the surgery was scheduled for June 1st. Both of us would have to do one more blood test seven days before the surgery date, along with a COVID-19 test to make sure nothing had changed. Thankfully, nothing changed, and we were set for surgery on June 1st, 2021.

I went down to Phoenix a week before the surgery to finish testing, and our town pulled through again with a honk-out for Tristan as he and his family left for Phoenix for the big transplant surgery. My family was blessed because several people had reached out and planned a meal train for them back home to ensure that they were taken care of while I was giving the gift of life. I had a chance to meet with Tristan, his mom, and his bonus dad the day before surgery and share some tears of joy and excitement with them. I also had the chance to interview with Fox 10 news. It was nerve-wracking, but I was thrilled to talk with them and spread awareness of living donation. I told them I had known and felt in the deep part of my soul that this was just going to be and that I needed to do whatever it took to get tested. I was excited to tell them I was going to share my spare in the morning. It felt like I was living in a fairy tale. Everything I had felt was going to happen was coming true. My heart was so deeply happy. On June 1st, 2021, I gave what I believed my grandmother had told me was my special gift.

Surgery went well, and both Tristan and I are doing great. I had expressed that all I wanted for my first meal after donation was a grilled cheese and tomato soup. When I was telling that to Tristan's mom, she said it was the same thing he wanted for his first meal as well. How fun to think we like some of the same foods now! As a thank you for being his donor, Tristan gave me a silver kidney bean from Tiffany's with our surgery date on it, along with a handwritten note that said, "Thank you for the kidney, you are my hero. Love, Tristan." I will cherish it forever.

As I reflect back on what I was able to do for this little boy, my heart is full. Tristan was finally able to return to in-person school. He was also able to play an entire season of baseball, and he was even invited to play for the All-Stars. When I attend school events for my children, it's always a nice surprise to see Tristan at the same events, enjoying life. Since he's in the same grade as my child, I have been able to watch him play in his orchestra concerts. I hear stories from his teachers, family friends, and his family about how different he is now, how they can't slow him down, how he's like a new kid. He can ride his bike for miles now without getting tired!

Watching Tristan live his best life was everything I had ever hoped and dreamed for him. I am so honored to know Tristan and his family now, and I feel like I have an extended family! We had an amazing opportunity in July of 2022, a year after the transplant, to be recognized by Donate Life Arizona at a Diamondbacks baseball game on the field. It was an amazing day that my family and I will never forget! Getting to spend time with Tristan's family, to meet his grandmothers and share tears of joy with them all, was such a special moment. We also got a nice surprise when the Mayor of Winslow, Roberta "Birdie" Cano, surprised us with her husband, Officer Cano, at the game. It was a humbling day, being surrounded by people that had been impacted by donation.

I can't wait to watch Tristan grow up and do all the things he dreams of doing, all because of organ donation! Following my calling was the best decision I ever made, even before I knew I was going to donate my kidney. I have already made my wishes known to my family that, when I pass away, I want to donate everything possible to help as many people as I can. I am so proud to call myself a living donor.

You can follow Tristan's story on the Tristan's Transplant Journey Facebook page.

About Harmony

Harmony Wells and her husband, Cliff, have been married for twenty-one years. They have four wonderful children together and five rescue kitties. Harmony was born and raised in Phoenix, Arizona, and she was blessed to have had an amazing relationship with her grandmother, Alice, who helped raise her.

Harmony is raising her children to think of others and to be actively involved in the community. She and her family donate to a lot of organizations, especially products from her business. Harmony's children enjoy the challenge every year to collect over two hundred canned goods for the local holiday food drive. During the last food drive, the boys went door to door and collected 268 cans.

As a child, Harmony remembers her grandmother telling her, "We all have special gifts to help people, and one day you will do great things." She has held that special message in her heart, but little did she know that one day she would do just that and more. Harmony is proud to know she saved a little boy's life and is now known as a town hero!

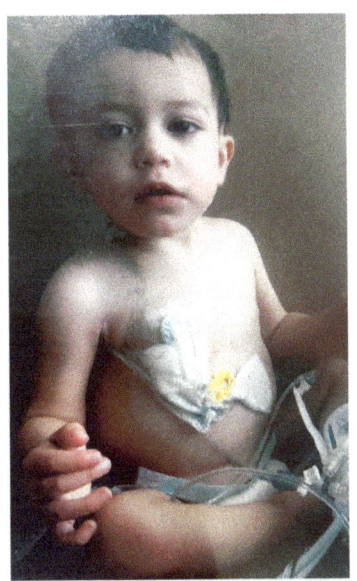
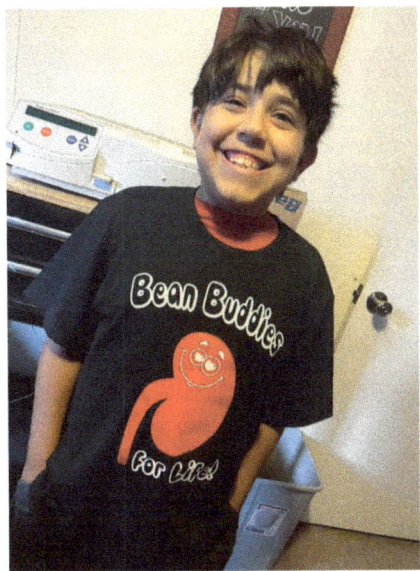

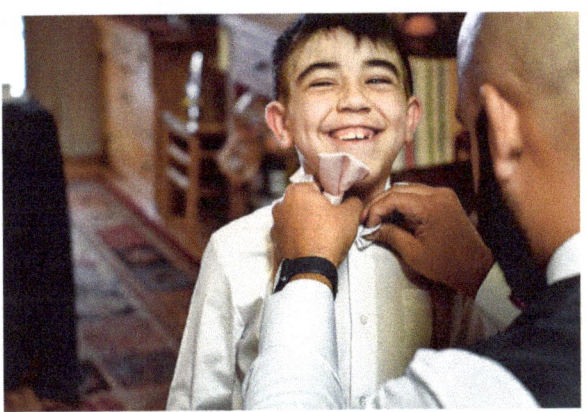

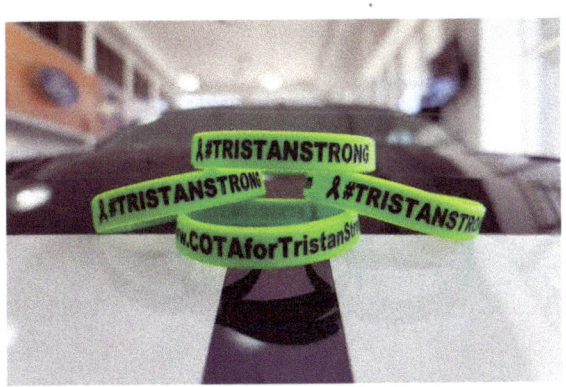

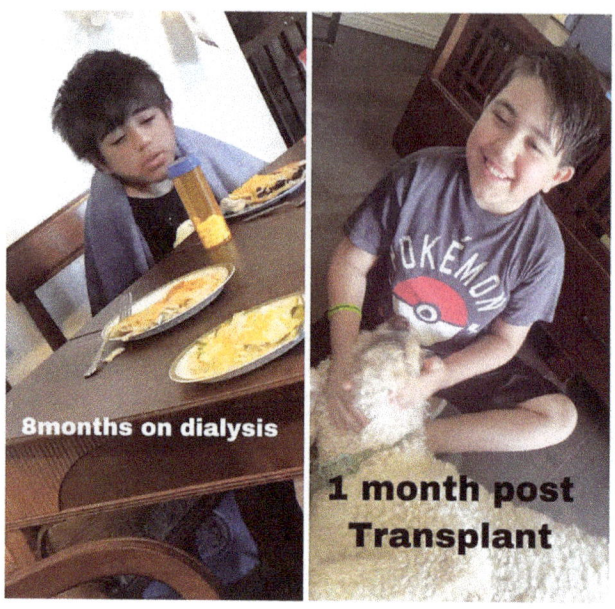

Tristan with his family and donor.

Tristan's donor.

Paying tribute to Tristan's donor.

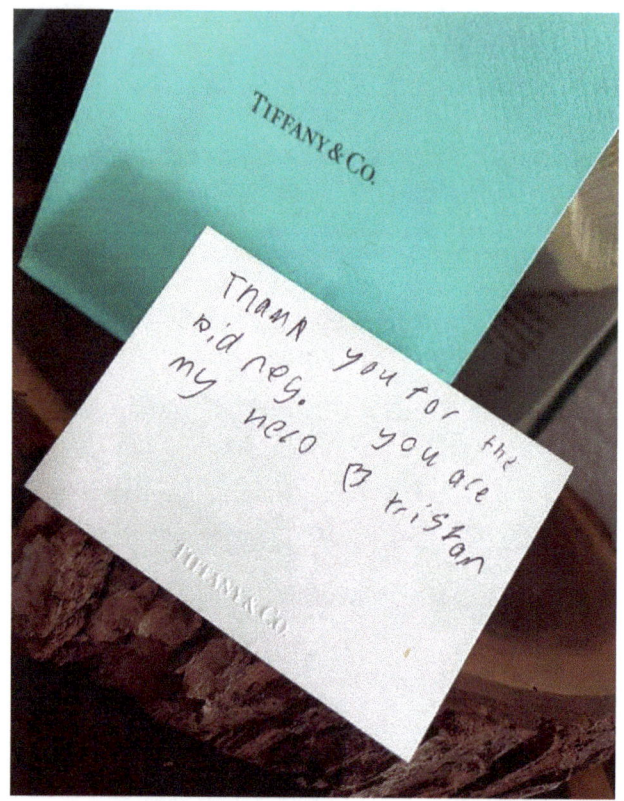

Thank you note Tristan wrote to his donor.

Tristan's first concert after his transplant.

Nathan's Journey

From Biliary Atresia to Liver Transplant

By Jen Lau

On December 29th, 2011, my husband and I were about to become a family for the first time. We packed up the car, stopped for a quick bite to eat, and checked into the mother-and-baby floor at Northwestern Medicine Delnor Hospital in Geneva, Illinois. The plan was to start induction that night and let Nate grace us with his presence. Little did we know, he had his own plan.

When Nate was born, everything seemed to be going well, but his skin was yellowing with jaundice. The nurses kept reassuring us this was normal and that we could put him in the natural sunlight to help it go away over time. We were new parents trying to figure out this new journey, so what did we know? They told us to follow up with the pediatrician per the schedule, and we were sent home as a family of three.

The first pediatrician visit went well. The doctor was pleased with Nate's weight, plus he was cooing, making wet diapers, and was a happy baby. Nate was still jaundice, and at that time, I was trying to breastfeed, so the doctor did mention that breastfeeding jaundice was normal. We went home thinking all was well.

As we started getting into a rhythm at home with a newborn, something seemed off to me. Nate became uncomfortable every time I went to feed him, and I noticed his stools were lighter in color. His yellow skin was not going away, and it even seemed to be getting darker. Then his eyes began to look yellow to me. I called the pediatrician's office, and I will never forget the answer I got from the nurse: They told me I was probably tired and overreacting, but if he was still not himself in a couple of days, I should call and make an appointment to be seen. While I felt like my concerns were being dismissed at the time, I agreed and waited. Things did not improve, so I called his pediatrician's office to be seen. Again, the doctor was pleased in general, but he put Nate on medication for GERD (gastroesophageal reflux disease), hoping this would help him be less fussy at feedings.

A couple of days passed, and not only was Nate getting fussier, but his jaundice was getting worse and his stools were getting lighter. He was inconsolable, and I felt that there was something truly wrong. I called the pediatrician's office to be seen, and they took us right away. When we arrived and were waiting in a clinic room, I asked the nurse why Nate was still jaundice. She still blamed it on the breastfeeding. When I told her I was not breastfeeding anymore, she gave me a look of concern and told me the doctor would be right in. A few moments later, he came in and told us that labs had been ordered. My husband and I walked down to the lab, and I just froze. I could not go in, nor could I watch. It is funny looking back on that decision now because I have watched countless lab draws and IV sticks. But at that moment, my heart could not do it. So, my husband took him in, and I sat outside, crying, as I heard Nate cry while getting poked.

Afterward, we walked back to the clinic room. Moments later the doctor came in, and his face said it all. I did not need him to explain Nate's labs. The stress in the room was high. He gave us the results and was very concerned this time. He wanted to get an ultrasound of Nate's liver to see if there was anything else going on, and he would call us at home with the results within hours. He did warn us that if they were to find anything, we would have to go down to Children's Memorial Hospital, so he suggested we pack a bag just in case. As we left the pediatrician's office, my heart sank. My husband did not say a word. We just held hands and walked out the double doors, holding our son.

Per the doctor's instructions, we showed up at the local hospital for an ultrasound. By this time, we had texted our parents to let them know what was going on. We entered the room, and the technician asked me if Nate had had any formula prior to the ultrasound. I nervously replied, "No." The technician began, but then said he was going to grab someone else, because he was having a hard time seeing Nate's gallbladder. He left us in the room, and there I was in a cold and loud room with a crying, hungry child. My anxiety levels began to soar. A couple of minutes went by, and the technician came back with another technician who then took more images, all while they both made sounds under their breath. I now know those sounds were not good sounds. We finished and headed home to wait by the phone for the results.

As we sat in the living room, our parents arrived to be with us. Nathan had been inconsolable all day and night, and he was not eating well. My husband kept his mind busy by watching mindless TV with our dads, while I sat in a chair and quietly stared at my phone. Our moms took turns holding Nate, giving him love and attention. They even got some giggles and smiles out of him. Finally, the phone rang. The pediatrician said that, based on the labs and the ultrasound, he wanted us to go down to Children's Memorial to see a specialist who treated liver diseases. He believed Nate was having an issue with his liver, and he was going to call down there to start the admission process for us. Someone would contact us soon. As I took notes, the tears poured down onto my paper, and I could not even see the writing. I hung up, went straight upstairs and packed.

Five West was the hospital floor that became our home. We were all checked in for the night, ready to take the next step to figure out what was wrong with our son. We met the medical team of doctors, who really took their time to educate us on Nate's possible diagnosis. They scheduled Nate for a liver biopsy first thing in the morning, but based on his lab reports and ultrasound, they felt he had a rare pediatric liver disease called biliary atresia. If so, the biopsy would confirm this. Biliary atresia (BA) is a condition in which the bile ducts are blocked, which prevents normal bile flow and causes damage to the liver. BA is life threatening without treatment. If Nate did have BA, he would need to undergo another procedure called a Kasai, which is a surgical treatment to try and help drain the bile to avoid causing further damage to the liver. If the Kasai was unsuccessful after three months, his liver would start to deteriorate, and a liver transplant would be needed to save his life.

Nate's liver biopsy did in fact show he had BA, and he ended up having the Kasai procedure at six-weeks-old. It was a long hospital stay, and the first of many to come with this disease. We made it home a month later, and my husband and I had to learn another "new normal" as parents.

Three months passed, and unfortunately, Nate's liver did not show the progress his team had hoped. The day my husband and I had feared the most had come; the medical team wanted to discuss a liver transplant. Hearing those two words together in the same sentence, liver transplant, broke my heart all over again. It felt like I had been kicked, after already being down. Unfortunately, with biliary atresia, a transplant was the only treatment that would save our son's life. We scheduled an appointment for his transplant evaluation and learned the good news that Nate was a good candidate for receiving a living donor liver transplant. His team of doctors informed us that a transplant from a living donor would be the best chance Nate would have for surviving his liver disease. Right away, we started identifying friends and family we thought might be suitable donors, and in that process, we also found complete strangers that were willing to help save Nate's life. We started sharing Nate's story and need for a liver transplant on social media, and had discussions with friends and family to help spread the word as well. It took us months to search for his perfect match.

While Nate was admitted for treating an episode of cholangitis (a serious infection of the liver's bile ducts), I received a phone call I will never forget. A dear friend of mine, Lori, called to tell me she had found out she was a match, and she wanted to be Nate's living donor. This was the first time I had exhaled in months. Tears full of so many mixed emotions filled my eyes. Even the nurses and doctors in the room with me at the time teared up, sharing the moment with me. After only two months of being listed, we found a donor, Lori was our hero, and Nate's guardian angel.

When Nate was nine-months-old, he and my dear friend, Lori, were ready for their big day. It was a long day of waiting, walking back and forth from Lurie Children's Hospital to Northwestern Hospital, checking on them both, and receiving updates from the medical team along the way. At last, Nate's surgeon came out to let us know that everything had gone as planned. Again, I was able to exhale. Lori's recovery went well. Since she was in her late twenties and healthy, her recovery took about six weeks, and she didn't have any complications. Lori has since gotten married, and she and her husband have two beautiful children. Nate is now 11-years-old and enjoying childhood and everything life has to offer at that age.

As a parent, nothing can prepare you for something of this magnitude. When you have a child, everything in the world is supposed to be right. Then, you blink, and you are standing in a children's hospital with doctors and nurses, your child hooked up to machines, and you are thrown into a journey of constant survival mode. Caring for a chronically ill child, whose outcome is unknown, leaves you emotionally and mentally exhausted. Then the heart-wrenching news that your baby needs an organ transplant is almost more than you can bear.

Going through this journey made me realize just how important pediatric organ donation truly is. In the moment, you are not aware of all the facts, such as donors needing to be appropriately matched by size, or that the supply of deceased donor organs for children is so small, leaving them more vulnerable to dying on the waitlist. Because of this, advocating for pediatric transplantation has become a passion of mine today. I have been able to take my own experiences as a parent, along with my son's experiences as a transplant recipient, and help others who are currently going through the same challenges. I've been able to help educate others on the importance of organ donation, how it gives children a second chance at life. Children need a voice, and as parents, we need to be that voice for them, especially for those children who are waiting for a life-saving gift, when the need for organs outmatches availability. I have met so many amazing families on this journey, and have learned so much working alongside some of the most amazing physicians and other advocates in our community. I give my gratitude to the physicians, surgeons, and the entire transplant community that advocates for children who must wait for that lifesaving gift, and for the parents who worry the gift will never come. It has been amazing to see the pediatric transplant community come together. I believe it takes a village to care for, and advocate for, children in this community. If we keep collaborating and maintaining a team-like approach in pediatric transplant medicine, the more our voices will be heard, and more positive changes for our children will happen.

Because of this journey, I decided to start my own organization, BARE: Biliary Atresia Research and Education. My vision in creating this organization was to not only advocate for more education and research that could lead to better outcomes in biliary atresia, but also to give a space for patients and families to feel supported, guided, and loved. Until BARE, there was not a single organization in the

U.S. for biliary atresia. I remember how scared and alone I felt when Nate was first diagnosed. I wanted to give parents like me a place where they could go and not have to feel the way I did ten years ago. BARE is currently collaborating with other key organizations in liver disease and transplantation on various projects, including its first ever educational symposium and the launch of a patient-focused biliary atresia registry. BARE is also involved in engaging with the community through social media and our own podcasts, and we are active in advocating for the awareness of organ donation.

Be an advocate for your child, or even someone's child you know, if you feel something seems off. Consider leaving a legacy as an organ donor, or even consider living donation. Because of organ donation, lives are saved, and the gift of life is passed on.

About Jen

Jen Lau is from Montgomery, Illinois and currently lives in the suburbs of Chicago. She has been married to Alex for ten years, and is mom to transplant recipient, Nathan (11), and to her daughter, Allyson (8). Jen loves to travel, write, and listen to music in her spare time.

Jen earned a B.A. in Mass Communication & Media Arts from Southern Illinois University Carbondale. She also attended Keller Graduate School of Management to complete master courses in Human Resources Management. Jen currently works for an IT company in the western suburbs of Chicago as a Human Resources Director and Office Manager. Jen has an extensive advocacy background in liver disease and transplantation. She has also served in leadership roles with SPLIT (Society of Pediatric Liver Transplantation), Starzl Network, and Transplant Families and Liver Mommas. She currently sits on the OPTN/UNOS Pediatric Committee and on the board at the Siragusa Transplantation Center at Ann & Robert H. Lurie Children's Hospital of Chicago as the patient/family advocate community member. Jen is also the founder and president of BARE: Biliary Atresia Research and Education.

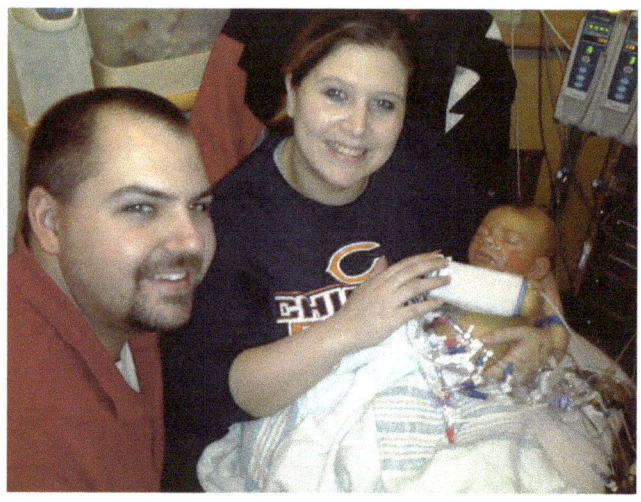

Nate when he was diagnosed.

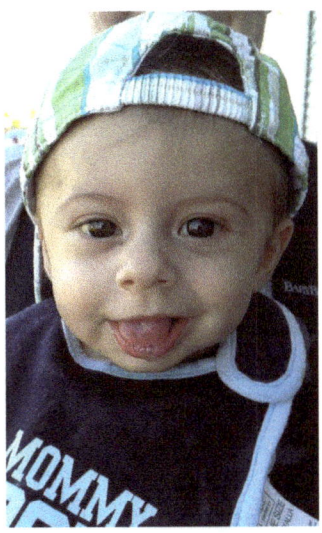

Nate pre-transplant.

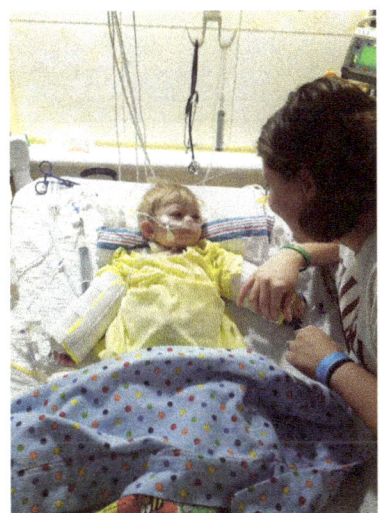

Nate after his transplant.

Nate and his donor, Lori.

Nate post-transplant, through the years.

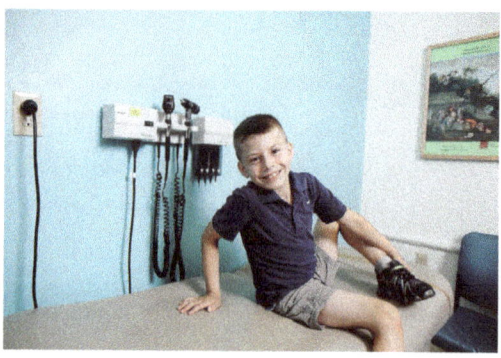

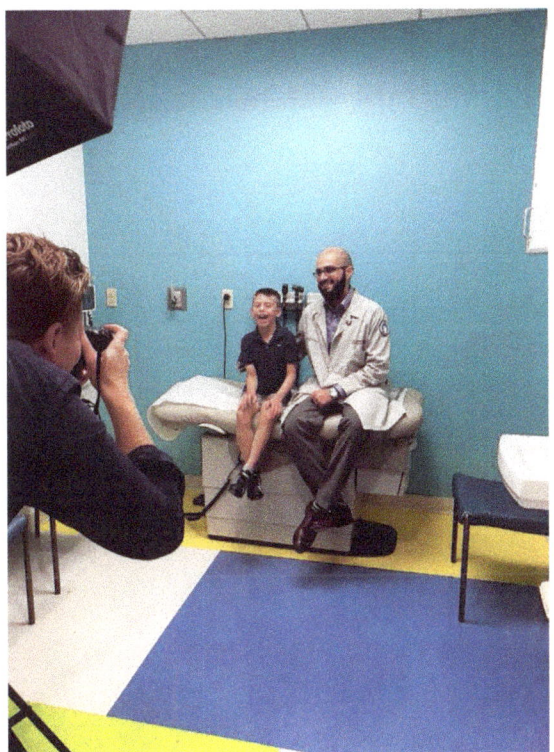

Nate with Dr. Mohammad for a photo shoot.

A Short Life,
but a Big Purpose

By Rachel Rodriguez

There comes a time in your life when you see your existence through a completely different set of eyes. Sometimes, through tragedy, you find a deeper appreciation for this thing called *life* and all that it throws at you: the good, the bad, the triumphant, and the life-shattering. There is purpose in what we endure, but the struggle is in reaching for the end of the tunnel with your senses, faith, and fortitude to persevere.

On March 29th, 2010, I became a first-time grandmother. My mother often shared that she loved me and my siblings endlessly, but there was something special about the love you have for your grandchildren. I never understood this until I held my first grandchild. Baby Malaikye stole my heart the moment I laid eyes on him. Ten little fingers, ten little toes. The beauty of God's special handywork was before my eyes. My love for him was instant; it was a new form of love as this baby was an extension of my youngest son, Daniel. As a father, my son was beaming with pride, and our lives became much fuller than we could have ever imagined. I looked forward to spending any time I could with my grandson. The camera constantly flashed when he was near. I was like a frenzied member of the paparazzi. At the time, I didn't know the importance of photographing special moments with him. A year later, I would fully understand.

My son Daniel's focus was on being a good provider and a good father. He had multiple jobs, often sacrificing a good night's rest to catch an early bus since he didn't have a vehicle at the time. Some days he would take multiple buses, leaving three hours before his shift started just to get to work on time. At the end of his shift, he went straight home to be with Kye (our nickname for Malaikye) and his girlfriend. Daniel's life was always centered around his baby. My mom and I were always happy to help with whatever was needed for baby Kye. That didn't happen often, but we sure jumped at the chance to help out when it did. We loved shopping for our newest little blessing.

Shortly before Malaikye turned one, my son and Malaikye's mother went through a breakup. Although their relationship was ending, his love for his son was stronger than ever. Daniel loved being a father. He made sure to discuss with her the importance of being allowed to remain in his son's life, and his desire to keep the bond he had with him. She agreed at first, but sadly things changed, and my son's time with Malaikye quickly dwindled. Daniel found himself in a fight to gain visitation rights. He was beginning the process to fight for his rights as a father through the court system.

Hospital

On August 13th, 2011, our lives took a shattering turn. I received a phone call that baby Kye was taken to the emergency room after an apparent fall. He was in a coma. The mother's boyfriend had been taking care of Kye and claimed that he fell from his toddler bed and hit his head on an alligator toy. I met my son on the pediatric intensive care unit (PICU) floor and checked in with the nursing staff. We asked if we could go in to see him, but we were told that the baby's parents were already in the room. Infuriated, my son said, "I am Malaikye's father!" Due to the issues of my son's rights as a father constantly being denied, I carried Kye's birth certificate in my purse. I quickly pulled it out and handed it to the nursing staff. Thankfully, they were very sympathetic and allowed us to enter the room. The last time my son and our family had seen Malaikye was at his first birthday party. He was happy, healthy, and full of life. To see him in these cold, unfamiliar surroundings was extremely painful. We both wept. My son was holding his baby's hand and trying to wake him. This is one of those memories deep within my soul that I will never forget. I remember looking at my grandson in disbelief. All I could think was, *How did this happen? Someone, please explain this!* Answers were not coming quickly enough. Soon after, we were taken into a room with a doctor and other medical staff who were concerned that Malaikye's injuries were not adding up to the story that was told to first responders and the sheriff's detectives.

A day passed and our sweet baby was not improving. I called our pastor and asked him to meet us in the PICU to pray over Kye. He quickly came, and we gathered alongside the crib to pray for a miracle that would breathe life back into our little one. Soon thereafter, doctors began to assemble in a room with Kye's mother and her family. Once again, my son was not included. He had every right to be present when they were giving an update on Malaikye's condition. As we had when we first entered the PICU, we fought to get Daniel in the room. He was told that the baby's mom did not want him in the room because her boyfriend was with her. Thankfully, the staff saw fit for Daniel to be present and invited him to the meeting. When he emerged from this meeting, he explained that two separate doctors would be running a series of exams to test whether or not Kye's brain was functioning at any level. If both doctors found no responses, then they would be declaring Kye brain-dead. They gathered both sides of Kye's family inside his room for the final test. Holding our collective breath, we waited. Zero brain activity. Our precious little one was declared brain-dead. All that we had prayed and hoped for was not going to be our reality. The medical team asked for a moment of silence in his honor.

My son and Kye's mother were approached by an organization called OneLegacy regarding the possibility of organ donation, something I am certain they had never really thought about before. They both agreed, and the paperwork was started. The search for recipients began in the hope of helping others in need. After spending days at the hospital, I was finally able to take my son home to shower and get some sleep. I don't believe any of us slept much that night. This nightmare was just starting, and it shook us to its core. Phones continued to ring as people were sending their love and condolences.

Early the next day, we were awakened by sheriff's detectives at our front door. They identified themselves as the detectives on Malaikye's case. We didn't realize at the time, but the moment our sweet boy was declared brain-dead, his case went from "accidental" to homicide. Someone was responsible for his death. Detectives now had the daunting task of trying to piece together what had happened. Anyone who had contact with Malaikye was listed as a suspect, questioned, and given a lie-detector test. The detectives believed that the account of what had happened, told by Kye's mother's boyfriend, was untrue. Being that Daniel was Kye's father, detectives wanted to question him regarding his relationship with Malaikye and his mother.

My son was open and honest. He explained the timeline and reasons for the breakup, and that he was being denied access to a relationship with his son. Daniel shared with them that even in the hospital, the staff had been told that the boyfriend was Malaikye's father. The detectives wanted to focus on the decision to donate Kye's organs, and they asked if my son had agreed to donate. He responded, "Yes, that's my signature." They went on to suggest that he should reconsider that decision, because removing the organs could tamper with any evidence that could be used to fight for justice. Daniel had never even thought of that, so he quickly changed his mind. He wanted whoever was responsible to be held accountable. The decision to donate came to a complete stop. The hospital called my son soon thereafter to ask us to come and say our final goodbyes since Malaikye would not be a donor. Malaikye was going to be taken off of life support. We all caravanned back to the hospital to say our final goodbyes to our precious little one.

Final Goodbye

Upon arriving at the hospital, I was approached and asked why my son had chosen to reverse his decision. I explained that the detectives had advised us that donating Malaikye's organs could tamper with evidence, and that we had every intention of seeking justice for Malaikye. In the hope that we would change our minds about donating, I was put in contact with the coroner's office so that they could explain the process. I spoke directly to the coroner, since my son was in no frame of mind to have that discussion. The coroner assured me that if he discovered any evidence in this case, he would not remove the organ. I was also assured that detectives would be in the room during the autopsy. With this important information, I asked for a confined room where my family could speak freely with Daniel.

At the end of the conversation, we assured Daniel that we would stand by him no matter what his decision would be. With tears in all of our eyes, we sat in silence while anticipating his decision, which was ultimately *yes*. He honestly just wanted something good to come out of this tragedy. Realizing that our little Kye could save lives and provide a second chance for others was comforting to him. Even though he was so little, he could do so much. Tears streamed down my son's face as he explained this to us. There would be no second birthday party, no school plays, no first dates, no wedding day. Malaikye's time here on Earth was ending, and so was a huge part of my son's life as he would never be the same again.

Once that decision was made, the hospital staff set aside time for Kye's parents to be alone with him. My son later shared with me that the nurses had disconnected some of the machines to allow him to hold Kye. They gently placed him in his daddy's arms. Daniel had longed to hold his son for six months but had been repeatedly denied that opportunity. Soft lullabies were playing in the background, but the room felt cold and empty, something Daniel had never felt before. He remembered the last time he spent with Malaikye; his first birthday party where Kye was placed on a pony, Daniel walking alongside him; the precious moment when baby Kye was feeding his daddy some birthday cake and smiling at him. But now, there was no life in him. I can imagine all the life events that Daniel had wished for his son were flooding his mind as tears flowed down his face.

When Daniel emerged from the other side of the double-doored PICU entrance, he came out a different young man: a broken, shattered man. My son collapsed on the floor in sheer grief. All I could do was run to him. On the floor, I held my boy and wept with him, praying for the Lord to help my son through this painful chapter of his life. Our family gathered in a waiting room to console Daniel. Nurses entered the room to ask who were the grandparents. I quickly rose and was led into Malaikye's room to spend my final moments with him. A gentle and kind-hearted staff member explained that she would be taking Kye's handprints and footprints for us, and a locket of his hair. She assured us that she would be very gentle. Standing there, looking at my beautiful grandchild, I was in awe at just how beautiful he truly was. He looked as if he were just asleep, but I knew he had already crossed over into Heaven. This beautiful staff member's name was Desiree, and I will always remember her. I took my grandbaby's hand in mine and took a final photo of that moment. Years later, Desiree and I would reconnect in a hospital waiting room. What an emotional reunion that was; she shared with me that, after Malaikye's passing, she asked to be reassigned somewhere other than on the PICU floor, as it was too emotional for her.

On August 15th, 2011, our Malaikye entered the gates of Heaven. But not before he was able to change the lives of four people in desperate need. Our baby was used by God to save the lives of four strangers. The reality of this is that God did grant a miracle that day. He granted four! He answered the fervent prayers of the parents, grandparents, sisters, brothers, and friends of these recipients. And for this, we are eternally grateful. Others did not have to suffer the loss of their family member.

The ages of his recipients ranged from nine months to sixty-five years. A nine-month-old girl received his liver. Sadly, her body rejected it, which happens at times. However, Malaikye was able to carry her to a second transplant. We are so grateful for that.

A two-year-old girl received his heart. Little Brooke was diagnosed with cardiomyopathy at two-months-old. Her heart was three times the size of a normal heart, making it too weak to pump blood properly. After two years of her condition being maintained with multiple medications, her heart had become too weak, and as a result, Brooke required a heart transplant at two-and-a-half years old. Today, she is living a happy and healthy life, which seems to have no limits for this beautiful young girl. Last May, at the age of thirteen, Brooke ran the Orange County Marathon, and just recently, she ran another half marathon, carrying our baby Malaikye for the ride of a lifetime.

All of the life experiences we wished our baby could have had, and Brooke is exceeding those experiences and making new memories with so many cheering her on, including our family. She is full of life and endless energy, and for this, we are so grateful that God chose her to carry our baby's heart.

A twenty-two-year-old college student received one of Malaikye's kidneys. Her name is Lorena, and she was diagnosed with kidney failure at the age of seventeen, right before her senior year of high school. She had been doing dialysis treatment for almost four years when she received the phone call that there was a match. Today, she is working at a museum, which she loves, and enjoying time with her family. She has shared with us that being healthy and taking care of Kye's kidney is what is most important to her. We are grateful to have a beautiful relationship with her and her family. The day Lorena received the call that a kidney was available happened to be her mother's birthday. Her mother, Maria, had one birthday wish as she blew out her candles: the wish was that her daughter would receive a kidney! This was a beautiful reminder of the importance of a wish, or a prayer, and a miracle from God.

The final recipient was a sixty-five-year-old woman. Sadly, she passed away many years ago, but baby Kye's kidney was able to provide her with a dialysis-free life during her final years, and more time with her family.

Our family is blessed and honored to have beautiful relationships with Brooke's family and Lorena's family. To be able to witness the lives they are living brings healing to our broken hearts. It is within their stories that we see hope after tragedy.

Fight For Justice

From day one of this journey, our family has been a testament to being a family of God. Where there was reason to unleash our anger towards all those responsible, we held our tongues. We knew that God would reveal all in His timing. On February 25th, 2014, our fight for justice came to an end. After three weeks of testimony, the jury returned a guilty verdict after deliberating for only four-and-a-half hours. The murderer was convicted of child abuse that had resulted in Malaikye's death. On April 9th, 2014, the murderer of our baby was sentenced to twenty-five years to life and now sits in prison. This person was Kye's mother's boyfriend, the very same person in the room when our baby was disconnected from the ventilator; the very same person who was given the rights as a father that my son was denied. A painful reality to this tragic story.

It was agonizing to remain restrained in a courtroom for all that time, but it was one of the truest of testaments that we can do all things through Christ who strengthens us! If it were not for our faith and our trust in God, this could have turned out so differently. We continued to walk confidently, fully knowing that God would administer justice according to His perfect will.

Today, the judicial part of the journey is over, and the murderer has been held accountable. For many, this loss would leave them numb and filled with rage, but I chose to persevere and find some positivity. I have chosen to honor my grandson's memory through acts of service. In his memory, I became a OneLegacy Ambassador. I am grateful to embrace a platform that gives me not only the chance to share Malaikye's story, but also to bring awareness to the beauty of organ donation. Yes, what happened to my grandson is another senseless story of child abuse, an epidemic plaguing our country, but on a positive note, he is also the face of hope offered through organ donation.

Today, we live life knowing justice was served for Malaikye. Our personal court journey may be over, but I continue to come alongside other families as they await their turn for justice. I just want to give back and invest my time in being of assistance whenever needed.

Daniel

My son Daniel is an amazing young man, who even with the constant pain of his loss, remains a young man of integrity, strength, and positivity. God has blessed him with a sense of renewed life in the form of the birth of his second son, Daniel Jr., and a daughter, Alyssa Marie. I believe it is not by chance that both of his children's birthdays are in the same month as baby Kye's anniversary in Heaven. I cannot put into words how very proud I am of my son. He and my daughter-in-law, Olivia, love their babies so very much. I remember after baby Kye passed away that my son told me he never wanted to have children again because the pain of losing Kye had crushed him. I told him not to think that way because he didn't know what the

Lord had in store for his future. I believe the Lord blessed my son for his selfless act of kindness to strangers in his darkest moment of grief.

Since Malaikye's passing, we continue to live life. It's not easy. Grief knocks on our door, and some days are harder than others. Days like Malaikye's birthday, or the anniversary of his passing, are still emotional and will be forevermore. I have made it my life's purpose to continue to share Malaikye and his story with whomever God has placed in my path. The day I held my grandson's hand for the last time, I made him a promise. That promise was to share his story of hope with others, even though the tears may fall. Being a part of this book is a fulfillment to the promise I had made to him.

As the anniversary of his passing approaches once again, we celebrate the life of a perfect little boy, one I was honored to be a grandmother to. Some ask, "How have you been able to endure such a horrific tragedy and keep your faith intact?" To this I reply, "I must remember that I am not alone, for the Lord is by my side. He has not forsaken me. He has guided me – without my being aware at times. I have seen and felt God in all of the ways that people have reached out to us and have felt strengthened by the numerous prayers lifted to the heavens on our behalf. He works through others to provide loving support, guidance, and healing. I have felt His comfort and remembered His promises, as I took one step in front of the other."

Malaikye's story continues to touch lives. It reminds us to hold our children tight and to not take a single moment for granted. We are never promised tomorrow. Our family's faith remains unshaken, because we know that it is only by the love, grace, and mercy of a powerful God that we can see the light of a new day, despite the grief journey we have endured. One sweet day I will hold my precious grandson Malaikye again when we are reunited in Heaven. Today is just one day closer to that day.

About Rachel

Rachel Rodriguez lives in Diamond Bar, California, and is a mother of two grown children, and grandmother of three. She is the owner of Sweets By La Rock where she specializes in custom cakes for every occasion.

In 2013, Rachel became a OneLegacy ambassador, and she embraces this platform to share the beauty of organ donation. Rachel has made it her mission to share her grandson's story, and to write about the hope that has come from the tragic passing of her grandson, Malaikye.

You can follow Rachel on Facebook and Instagram:
@SweetsbyLaRock.

In 2008, baby Malaikye was honored with a Floragraph
on the 2008 Donate Life Rose Parade Float.
Pictured here, alongside me, is Lorena Lopez. She is one
of Malaikye's kidney recipients.

Miss you my angel Kye in the Sky.

*Lorena, kidney recipient.
Living a happy and healthy
life due to the beauty of
organ donation.*

Safe in his Daddy's arms.

As a One Legacy Ambassador, I share Malaikye's story with others coming to see the float. This woman shared with me that her son had passed away and was a donor. All I could do was hold her.

Fellow OneLegacy Ambassadors: Margaret Gonzalez & Carol Rivera, sharing the importance of organ donation at the Donate Life Rose Parade float in 2023.

A photoshopped gift I gave to my son, Daniel, for Christmas. The child on the left is baby Malaikye. Danny Jr and Alyssa are to the right. All three babies together.

Malaikye is lighting up the
Heavens with his contagious smile.

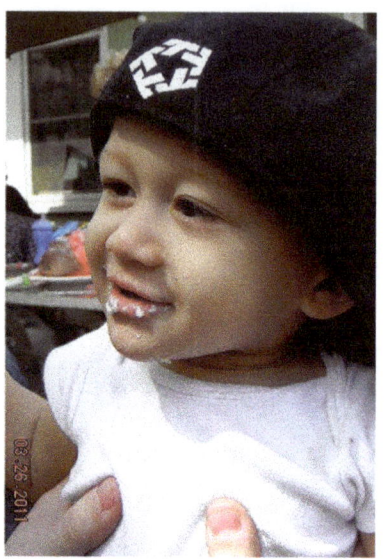

Baby Malaikye smiling as he
and Daddy ate birthday cake.

Daniel and his precious little boy.
Daniel absolutely loved being a father.

Malaikye's 1st Birthday

*Little brother, Danny, honoring his
big brother, Malaikye, at the Donate
Life Run/Walk in Fullerton.*

Daniel, Olivia, Danny, and Alyssa.
My son's blessings from God.

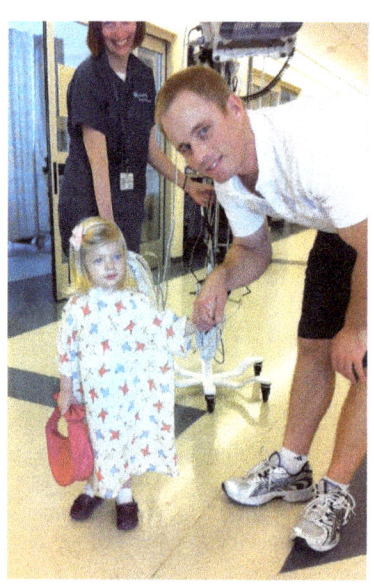

August 20, 2011: Two days after her heart transplant, Brooke did a lap with her daddy around the PICU and then asked to go again.

Brooke reaching new milestones everyday thanks to the beauty of organ donation and the gift of a new heart!

Ava's Miracle

By Tom Schaefer

BACKGROUND

The Schaefer journey dates back to 1999, when our oldest daughter, Alaina, checked into an emergency room (ER) in Appleton, Wisconsin, and they determined she was "full of kidney stones." It was the first of many blessings in disguise that we had during this journey, because the on-call urology doctor, Dr. Chybowski, who treated her, ended up being our urologist until his retirement in 2018.

Alaina underwent a procedure to break up the stones after this visit. In our search for a nephrologist, we found that the Mayo Clinic in Rochester, Minnesota, had one of the top pediatric nephrologists in the world, Dr. Milliner, who was willing to take on our four-year-old daughter as a patient (blessing number two).

Biannual trips to Mayo began for our family; my wife, Amy, myself, Alaina, and our two-year-old, Alexandra. Alaina was diagnosed with a liver disorder called primary hyperoxaluria type 1. We call it PH1, and it is about as rare of a disorder as you can get. During these trips, blood draws, ultrasounds, and CT scans were typically the first order of business. The Mayo Clinic is an impressive place. As a massive beehive of daily activity, there are thousands of doctors, nurses, technicians, and support staff helping thousands of patients from around the world each week. Since PH1 is so rare, and there are no known cures or medications to take, the best thing we could do for Alaina was maintain her kidneys by pushing fluids as often as possible.

During a trip to Mayo in the summer of 2001, our five-month-old, Ava, was tested. Her readings were off the charts, which meant she too had it. This also meant our appointments would now be doubled, as both girls would need to be seen. In terms of the severity of the disorder, our girls fell somewhere in the middle, with their main issue being kidney stones.

Amy's games bag was always close by, which certainly helped the girls occupy a lot of downtime between appointments and tests. Our two rock stars, however, were Alaina and Ava. They had to deal with bloodwork, tests, appointments, and endless questions about how they were "doing." I have always believed that their maturity levels, compared to that of their peers, was a direct result of them having to experience adult things at a very young age.

As the Schaefer family continued to grow (our daughter, Audra, was born in 2006), the events with PH1 usually involved kidney stones that were handled locally, and our trips to Mayo were pared down to once a year. The girls continued to lead, for the most part, healthy and active lives.

2017: A Year to Remember

Fast forward to March 2017. Ava was experiencing kidney stone pain, which resulted in the usual ER visit, bloodwork, procedure, recovery, and bounce back to pre-stone levels. Except not this time. Dr. Chybowski was concerned that Ava's creatinine (the blood waste product that filters through the kidneys) was significantly higher than previous readings from a year ago. I think, for the first time, we realized that the events we had been dreading were finally at hand. A weekend of fluids did not improve her results, so we made a one-day trip to Mayo to formally begin the transplantation process.

Unlike Alaina's progression through PH1, Ava's was more of a slow deterioration of her kidney function. This latest stone episode had probably exacerbated the problem. At that point, we moved from MAINTENANCE to TRANSPLANTATION. Blessing number three: Ava was still considered a pediatric patient, so she automatically moved up the priority list for transplants. Blessing number four: If a transplant was in the cards for Ava, the timing was right since she was almost an adult but still considered a child, and she had sixteen years to "build her immunity and body up."

The process of bloodwork, tests, and meetings began in earnest the last week of April 2017. I think I can speak for Amy and Ava when I say that our heads were swimming by the end of the "orientation." As we walked through the now-familiar subways, skyways, and halls that connected all of the offices and destinations that we needed to get to, we passed thousands of people. In our minds, we couldn't believe that there were people worse off than us, but seeing all of the various visible struggles of people of all ages snaps you back to reality and puts your "world" a little more into perspective. I knew Ava was not the first, nor will she be the last, sixteen-year-old needing a transplant; it just felt that way in the moment.

Ava's oxalate, which is the stuff our liver produces but can normally get rid of through our kidneys (PH1 patients produce too much of it), had increased considerably. Ava was going to require hemodialysis to remove the excess oxalate that her body was not getting rid of fast enough. We were floored to find out that she would need dialysis this quickly. Ava and I headed back to Mayo on May 3rd for a week, to have a catheter placed in her chest for dialysis, and to see how she would respond. We settled into our new "normal" at the hospital with blood tests and a full round of dialysis. Ava was a champ and very polite, despite all of the people in and out of her room and having to repeat her name and birthdate several times a day.

The goal for that trip was to determine how quickly Ava's oxalate levels would bounce back to high levels once they had been lowered through dialysis, and to also see how many rounds of dialysis per week she would need when we got home. The amount of blood they took brought on another worry: anemia. The decision was made to scale back on the bloodwork.

Fortunately, Ava and I didn't have to be alone at Mayo for long. The entire family was coming to visit. Alaina was the first to arrive, and it was clear that Ava was happy to see her. The rest of the crew from Wisconsin came shortly after; Grandma, Grandpa, Mom, Dad, Ava and her three sisters, and the tech were all in a room that was meant to hold far less people. We all left except for Alaina, who helped Ava shower.

Sitting in the chapel early the next morning at Mass, I was struck by the Gospel (John 10:1–10) about Jesus the Good Shepherd and how, if his flock is "lost," they can fall prey to others. I didn't know how well the analogy fit in our situation, but I think if we can continue to have faith, we will be ok… A comforting thought. In my heart, I know I have to have faith that things will all work out even when it does not appear that way.

The updated status that we were given as we prepared to head home was: dialysis would most likely be needed six times a week. This meant thirty-plus hours per week devoted to dialysis would be our "new normal." Dialysis centers are rare for pediatric patients, so Children's Hospital in Milwaukee was likely our only option.

We received some disheartening news regarding living donor possibilities for Ava: Due to her rather unusual situation, doctors determined that, at this point, Ava's donation should come from a deceased donor so that both the full liver and kidney could be transplanted in her. At minimum, I hoped that this determination sparked a conversation about organ donation in general for all of the people who had inquired about potentially being Ava's living donor. It was very difficult, however, to wrap my head around the fact that for Ava to have a "normal" life, another family would have to deal with a death. Once again, this put our world in perspective.

Summer 2017

We settled into our driving arrangements routine for Ava's dialysis. The biggest challenge was scheduling around Ava's schedule. Aside from being tired, she had been able to do most things. We tried to keep things as normal as possible with our family during this time. While we were hoping to get a call soon for transplant, we were happy that Ava was healthy other than the obvious. We continued to be amazed at all the support we received to make our lives easier. Our daughter, Audra, and a friend set up a "LemonAVA" stand, which was a big hit.

At this point, Ava had been on dialysis for a little more than three months. She was in good spirits, and we continued to make it as normal of a summer as possible for our family. Ava worked part-time at Ponderosa, and she also played tennis! We were able to work around her dialysis schedule to make most practices and matches.

This is Not a Drill

Audra came running down the stairs late on September 1st, 2017, wide-eyed, saying Mom was on the phone with a doctor. I ran upstairs to find Amy shaking. "They would like us to get to Rochester by 6:00 am. WE HAVE A MATCH." I couldn't believe what she had just said. I felt an odd calm wash over me as I threw a few clothes together, organized some things, and called my parents to come over. We discussed the plan of attack. In the meantime, Ava was at the varsity football game and would be going to a neighbor's house for a bonfire afterward, so she wasn't even home! We decided to let her enjoy her night before telling her the big news. She was a little bit shocked by the news when we did tell her, but she got her things packed and was ready to go.

We pulled out of our driveway at 1:52 am. The adrenaline was pumping, but I will tell you, the endless orange construction cones we passed were hypnotizing. It felt like the longest trip we had ever made up to Mayo in Rochester. We arrived at the ER at 5:45 am to an unsuspecting staff. I was already making calls to Children's Hospital to cancel Ava's dialysis, to the Ronald McDonald House to set up accommodations, and to our insurance company. Around 7:30 am, we finally made our way to the Pediatric ICU. A doctor informed us that they would still do dialysis that morning. Ava took a shower, and we went to get a quick bite to eat. The transplant wasn't going to take place until at least 7:30 pm. The surgeon estimated five to six hours for the surgery. I imagined that the behind-the-scenes coordination of this "event" was tremendous. "Gonna Fly Now" was the theme song we had chosen for Ava as we waited for the procedure. For those who don't know, that is the theme song from the movie *Rocky*.

Ava got into her waiting wheelchair at 7:35 pm. We could finally exhale for a little bit. As a friend put it, this was Ava's "second birth." Ava began her life at 3:30 am on February 23rd, 2001, so the significance of her second "birth" beginning in the wee hours of the morning, between September 2nd and 3rd, 2017, was not lost on me.

SUCCESS!

At about 3:00 am, Ava got back to her room, with no fewer than ten nurses and doctors checking everything out. She had officially begun receiving her organs around 10:00 pm. She received her liver first, on September 2nd, and the kidney on September 3rd. The doctors were very happy with how everything had gone, and her new organs were functioning properly. At 5:30 am, Ava had the breathing tube removed as she slowly woke up from the procedure. Then post-operative pain kicked in. It's hard to describe watching your daughter barely speak above a whisper because her throat is sore from the breathing tube, eyes closed, and wincing because of the pain during movement. It broke me watching her cry when lines were moved around, or a clot pushed through a drain tube, or the crazy itching because of the steroids. Our poor daughter had hot flashes from the fentanyl; she was experiencing chest pains from the fluid in her lungs and not being able to fully inhale because of the sutures from her surgery.

Ava's recovery was slow and steady. She started with a few steps out of her room and down the hall. The medical team said the more she moved, the better she would feel. It was heartbreaking to watch her struggle the few days after transplant, but we continued to have faith and hoped that the small steps would soon become big steps.

Out of the Hospital

Ava's hospital stay was less than eleven days. In that time, Ava had been given a second chance for a "normal" life, thanks to the selfless gift of organ donation from a family we may never come to know, but to whom we will always be eternally grateful.

It was an exhilarating, nerve-wracking, emotional, painful, exhausting couple of weeks. But visits from family and from her older sisters made things more tolerable for Ava. Before we could actually leave and settle in at the RM House for post-op recovery, we needed to get "educated" on our "new normal": life after transplant. Ava was a little reluctant to be discharged; she would be starting out in a whole new world, and the safety net of the hospital, while only a few blocks away, seemed like a million miles.

We learned that this particular transplant was NOT as common as one might think. There had not been a pediatric liver-kidney transplant at Mayo for at least eight years. That is one of the many reasons why I firmly believed Ava was the strongest and bravest sixteen-year-old I knew. I found a quote in the hospital gift shop that said, "Do not tell GOD how big your STORM is, tell the STORM how big your GOD is." That resonated. Our faith, and all the prayers and support from those around us, really helped us weather the storm.

After leaving the hospital, pain management seemed to be the biggest issue for Ava. Pain, nausea, anti-rejection, anti-fungal, and antibacterial medications were on her list. We decided that, in order for Ava to feel more like Ava, she needed to wean herself off of the stronger pain meds and work harder to move more and drink more. Those were her best options for feeling better sooner. She thankfully improved to the point of taking only Tylenol as needed.

Another offshoot of being on many medications is Clostridium difficile (more affectionately known as C. diff). We are fairly certain that the "plumbing" issues Ava was having early on after discharge was this, but with diarrhea being a side effect of many of the medications, it was difficult to know where or when the issues had originated. Anybody who has had this also knows your home becomes a whole new adventure in disinfecting as well! Ava slowly got her appetite back, and she moved from wheelchair service to walking. Her posture straightened back "up" to her normal 5'8". She was also back to her pre-transplant weight of around 59 kg. On September 9th, her weight was 71.3 kg because of the meds and the excessive amounts of fluids she was getting. This equated to about 27 pounds, gained and lost, in about four weeks.

Homework, visits from friends, a team video, and T-shirts from teammates were all part of the new normal for Ava as she recuperated at the RM House. There were some long days at the clinic, but fortunately, Ava was able to tolerate it because she was feeling better daily.

Ava went for her last labs and was told by the liver and kidney teams that, if the labs were all clear and everything went as planned, they would give their blessing for us to head home a few days earlier than we had originally thought. Not everything went quite as planned due to the vicious cycle of medications that seemed to "set off" other meds, but the hope was that being in her own home, and in her own bed, would aid her return to normalcy. We finally made it home late on October 6th. Amazingly, our time from transplant to back home was thirty-five days.

Reflection

There has been much to take in and reflect on throughout this journey. *Ava* has been the star. If there was anyone stronger or more courageous during this time, you would have had a hard time convincing me.

Amy, who divided her time between work, home, and Mayo, kept everything running smoothly back in Wisconsin, even though her heart was always in Minnesota.

While our youngest, Audra, did not quite understand all that had gone on, she missed her sister. She was present off and on for the first month of fifth grade. Our two oldest, Alaina and Alexandra, helped out immensely, mainly by being there several times for Ava, and sharing some very profound thoughts on their own social media posts about this experience from their perspective.

Friends and family were and continue to be our support system; we can never thank them enough. And finally, the donor, who either at her own choosing or her family's, made the selfless decision of organ donation. Even the little things, like a former tennis opponent of Ava's, whose first ever check was written to support Ava, or the priest at the chapel who prays for Ava every day, puts life into perspective when we reflect on this chapter in our lives.

Post-Transplant

It took roughly one month for Ava, once we got home, to feel well enough to see people, be seen in public, do homework, and so forth for more than just a brief time. As I told most people, "It will be a marathon, not a sprint." The biggest leap for Ava was getting back to school, part-time, and then eventually full-time. Attending events and socializing with friends also became a regular part of life for her again.

Despite all these wonderful strides, we still had to worry about germs and sickness. As a transplant patient, Ava is more susceptible to catching something due to her immunosuppressed state. She is also limited to what medications she can take when she does get sick, since she cannot compromise her anti-rejection medications.

Ava and I arrived back at Mayo, one week earlier than our scheduled four-month checkup, because her creatinine levels had crept back up. Thankfully, they did return to "baseline." Her four-month checkup came and went with some very encouraging signs. Ava had not really exhibited any signs of rejection at this point, and the scheduled biopsies confirmed this. At this checkup, I was reminded of the second lease on a "normal" life that she had been given by her donor and the incredible decision that the donor's family had made. I was also reminded weekly, when Ava and I went to the hospital for follow-ups, to ensure the health of her new organs. Prescriptions and lab numbers, although cumbersome, help her and also help her doctors gain a better understanding of Ava moving forward.

As we began 2018, we were cautiously optimistic, but realistic that there would be some more wrinkles to iron out as we continued to celebrate milestones in Ava's post-transplant life. These milestones were not by days and weeks anymore, but by months and years, which was another reminder of how far Ava had come.

Ava went in for her outpatient biopsy procedure as part of her four-month checkup. Ironically, her recovery room was in the "transplant wing" of the Pediatric ICU. A flood of memories from that period in our journey opened up. The room next to Ava back in September was occupied by a little dark-haired boy. He had been placed in the room the same day that Ava was moved to her room. Four months later, the little boy was still there, sans hair, and confined to that room. It broke my heart that we were fortunate to "move on," and he was not. Again, the realities of life were much more magnified and apparent when our "problems" pale in comparison to others.

Appointments and checkups with each team took up portions of the next two days. In between, we made a stop at the Ronald McDonald House to exchange quick hellos with the staff and to deliver a sign, "HOME SWEET HOME," that I had made for the house.

Transplant Plus One Year

Ava and I were back at Mayo for her one-year checkup and biopsies. We saw the same rooms and the same faces, and experienced the same protocols that had been such a big part of our lives in September and October of 2017. Ava's former room was now occupied by an infant, probably no more than six months old. The sign next to the door read "Caution: Chemotherapy Treatment." Every new occupant faces a new challenge. I reflected back on fourteen months ago, on how our daughter was given the gift of a new life from an unknown donor, but we were still in "shock and awe" mode, looking at her attached to so many tubes and machines.

Ava was progressing well and continued to be weaned off of some of the medications prescribed post-transplant. The team was very optimistic about her progress.

Ava was able to get back to a normal schedule academically and socially. From a medical standpoint, her transplant and recovery were fairly uneventful. She received news early in 2018 that her Make-A-Wish choice of visiting Hawaii would be happening. Ava definitely deserved this! Later in the spring, she was voted to the Junior Prom Court, culminating in Ava being crowned Queen. It was bittersweet, as the long day of pictures, travel, and dinner took its toll, and Ava had to cut short her post-prom festivities.

Tennis dominated the latter part of the summer and early fall, as Ava began her senior year and was on the number one doubles team. Ava being able to play was nothing short of a miracle, but being able to play at a high level, which ultimately ended in Ava and her partner advancing to the State level, was a storybook ending. I had to catch myself sometimes when she was not playing well, or missing shots that she should have made, and remember the "big picture" of where we were one year ago. In addition to her amazing accomplishments in tennis, Ava was also awarded a state-level Perseverance Award!

The Letter

On November 12th, as we were having an annual checkup at Mayo, I received a call from our Mayo connection to LifeSource, the organ procurement organization for Minnesota, the Dakotas, and Western Wisconsin, telling me that we had a letter from Ava's donor family.

I saw Ava off to her procedure and headed to the dimmed chapel to read the note. As I began reading, the space became flooded with light; the sun was finally showing its face after two days of dreariness. It streamed through the stained glass, almost as if someone knew I was reading the note at that time.

We could now put a name to Ava's donor: Taryn.

September 3rd, 2022

As we reflect on where Ava was in 2017, compared to where she is today, and how many people made a difference to make that a reality, we are blessed. Certainly, it was not all smooth sailing, but Ava was remarkably resilient, battling various ailments and side effects of the different changes and medications. We are so proud of the strong advocate she has become for herself, especially when dealing with the multitude of health care professionals over the last few years.

Our family has been blessed with graduations, vacations, and the wedding of our oldest daughter, Alaina. Ava has been able to share in the joys of Schaefer life events while maneuvering through her own. All things considered, it has been a pretty great five years. Of course, every anniversary is bittersweet as it is also a reminder that another family is marking that day for a different reason. They can be secure in the knowledge that their selfless decision, the gift of organ donation from their precious daughter, sister, granddaughter, niece, cousin, and friend has allowed others to continue to mark milestones in their own families.

How can you adequately quantify that gift? A million thank you's don't do it justice. Because of organ donation, the greatest gift was given to our family five years ago, and we can never repay that except to try to live up to the standards of Taryn, our forever angel.

Ava will be graduating from the University of Wisconsin-Oshkosh in the Fall of 2023. She has looked into the role of child life specialists, and other health-related field careers, where her experiences would most certainly prove a worthy resource. Alaina is expecting her first child in May of 2023. Her health has continued to be stable, and we are praying for an "uneventful" pregnancy. There is the potential for changes in PH1 patients after physical changes in their bodies occur. She has been very fortunate thus far, but the possibility of transplantation still exists, as the cure for PH1 is an elusive one.

We have communicated with Taryn's family a few times via mail and Facebook, although we have been reluctant as we are experiencing "survivor's guilt." We have followed the family on social media. They advocate for organ donation, and they have a mission called "Taryn's Trail," which is a message to "spread love, grace, and kindness." They were pleased that we wanted to include Taryn's pictures in our chapter.

About Tom

Tom has been in education since 1991 and is currently teaching in the Special Education Department at Hartford Union High School in Hartford, Wisconsin. In the past, he has worked in construction, coaching, and mentoring. Tom has been a school board member and has also worked as an adult tennis league coordinator. He currently serves on his church's parish board, ushers for the church, and is a caretaker for his local parish cemetery. At the high school, Tom works as a game manager, clock operator, and announcer for most sports.

Amy, Tom's wife of thirty years, is a 4K teacher in the Honor School District. Their oldest daughter, Alaina Merrick, and her husband, Kyle, live in St. Paul, Minnesota. The family celebrated their wedding in August 2022, and Tom and Amy are anxiously awaiting their first grandchild in May 2023! Alexandra is a traveling sonographer currently living in Sheboygan, Wisconsin, with her boyfriend, Mitchell. Ava, the star of the show, is finishing up her studies in psychology at the University of Wisconsin-Oshkosh, with an expected graduation date in December of 2023. Audra is currently a sophomore in high school. She enjoys tennis and track, and working at her first job at Starbucks!

Tom enjoys watching movies and sports, reading about history, working outside, learning about genealogy, and working with young people. He is an advocate for organ donation and has his own backstory. Chad Farner, of Oskaloosa, Iowa, is now a happily retired educator, thanks to Tom's lifesaving gift of bone marrow in 2005.

Writing this chapter, which was taken in part from Tom's various blogs during the critical period leading up to, and during, Ava's transplantation, was a form of catharsis for Tom, as he has shared his thoughts and feelings during this momentous time in his family's life.

You can connect with Ava on Instagram: @avaschaefer

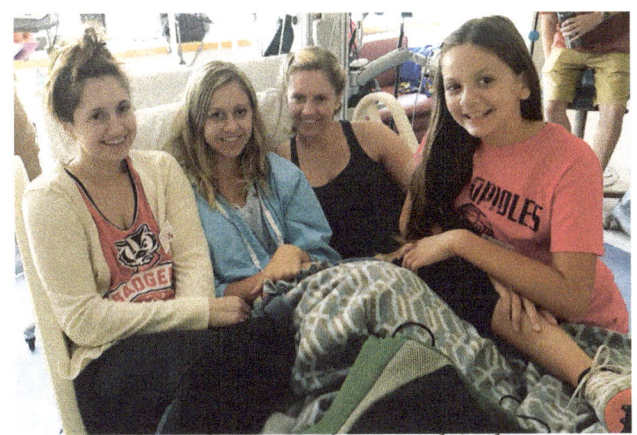

Alexandra, Ava, Alaina, and Audra,
September 2, 2017, a few hours before surgery.

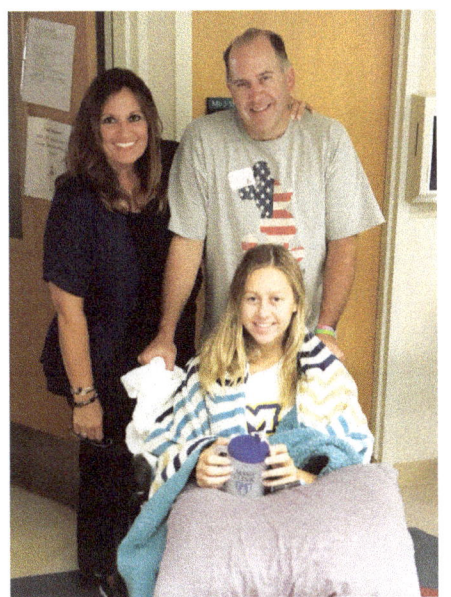

Mom, Dad, and Ava.

Ava-5th Anniversary of her kidney-
liver transplant, September, 2022,
Oshkosh, Wisconsin.

Make-A-Wish trip to Hawaii,
June, 2018. She enjoyed zip-
lining, hiking, a helicopter
ride, snorkeling, and a luau.

Ava visiting Rochester, Minnesota. Summer, 2018.

Alaina Schaefer/Kyle Merrick Wedding, Hastings, MN, August 5, 2022. Dad (Tom), Audra, Mom (Amy), Alaina, Kyle, Mitch Datka, Alexandra, and Ava.

Ava, at the Pier, 2021.

Dad, Mom and Ava celebrated with other transplant recipients back in Rochester, Summer, 2018 at the annual Transplant Reunion.

Ava, 2021.

Ava doing a "Homecoming" shoot, Mayo style, less than 4 weeks post-transplant. Plummer House, Rochester, Minnesota.

Christmas at the Schaefer's, 2022.
Mitch, Alexandra, Coder, Audra, Mom, Dad, Kyle, Alaina, and Ava.

Ava, Hartford Union High School Prom Queen, April, 2018.

Taryn Dalain Paul-January 5, 2002-September 1, 2017. The Schaefer Family's Forever Angel. Two others were saved by her gift of organ donation.

"What we do for ourselves dies with us, what we do for others remains and is immortal."
– Albert Pine

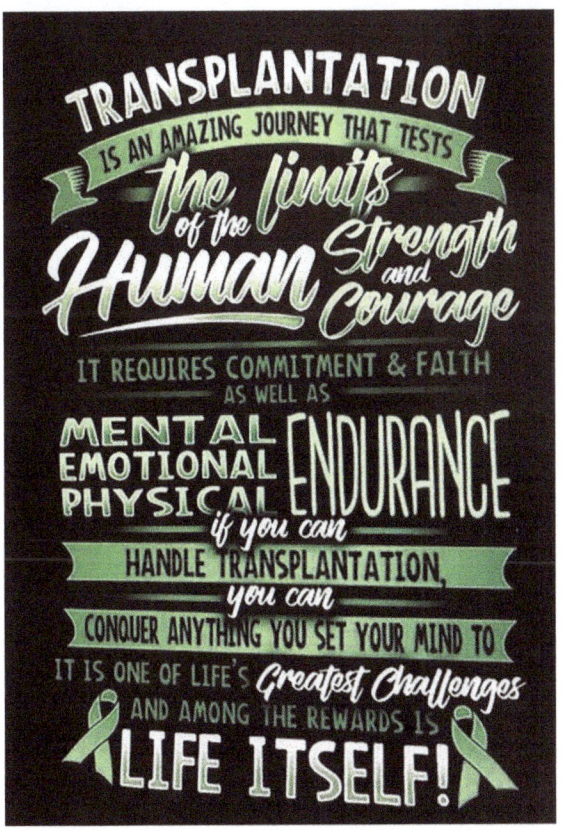

Do it for Dom

By Sara Snider

I was 17 years old, single, and two weeks past my due date when I walked into the hospital to have my labor induced. My mother and oldest sister were by my side the entire 26-and-a-half hours of labor and delivery. On June 28th, 1996, I gave birth to my son, Dominic Michael Hooper, and instantly, my life changed. Dominic (Dom) had finally given me a reason to exist in this world. I struggled, adapting to my new role as a mom, but with the help of my family, I found my path and my purpose. Dominic and I basically grew up together. During his childhood years, we lived in our small hometown of Scott City, Missouri, where most of my family resides. I know without a doubt that I would not have been able to grow up, plus raise my son, without the help of my supportive family. For years, it was just Dom and me living day to day, trying to figure out life. In 2006, I was offered a job advancement that required us to move to Northeast Tennessee for a year. I truly believe that year brought us closer together as mother and son. We both had a hard time, missing our family and friends, but that separation helped us rely on each other more. When we returned to Scott City, I purchased a house, and we finally had a place we could call home. Dominic attended grade school at a local Catholic school, just a block from our house. He loved sports and spent much of his time playing basketball, volleyball, and baseball during grade school.

In 2008, I met a man named Chris, who was from Kentucky. We started talking and got to know each other. He made several trips to

Missouri to spend time with Dominic and me. As our relationship grew, Chris and I discussed him moving to Missouri to live with us. I remember the day that I sat down and talked with Dom, to ask him how he felt about Chris moving in. Since it had always been the two of us, I knew there would be some adjusting, and I had to be sure my son was all right with this big change. Once we had Dominic's blessing, Chris made the move to Missouri, and we were married in March of 2010. My main requirement for our wedding was that Dom walk me down the aisle and give me away. Our family of two grew to include Chris and his two children, Amanda and Drake, who live in Kentucky. Chris immediately accepted Dom as one of his own, providing a much-needed male role model and father figure. He was the basketball coach during Dom's eighth-grade year and worked with him tirelessly to perfect his basketball skills.

High school came around, and Dominic became involved in more school sports: football, weightlifting, basketball, and baseball. I watched with amazement as he transformed his chubby, youthful physique into a toned, muscular teenage body. Dom was very active in sports, got great grades, and was taking dual college courses. He was accepted to attend Southeast Missouri State University to study as an electrical engineer. Sports were Dom's passion, and he gave 100% in every one he played. Chris and I could be found on the sidelines of the court, or field, watching Dominic play. I attended all of his games and can honestly say I was his number-one fan.

Amidst all the sports and games, Chris would still make time every other weekend to make the five-hour drive each way to see his kids in Kentucky. On February 21st, 2014, Dom was in his senior year, three months away from graduation. Chris was on his way to Kentucky when Dominic came home from school that day. He was very excited as he and some of his friends had made plans to ride their four-wheelers. He came in, changed his clothes, and was headed out the door when I stopped him and told him to be careful. He smiled and said, "I will, Mom." I watched as he ran down the hill and jumped into his friends' truck to go pick up his four-wheeler. Two hours later, I would receive the phone call that would irrevocably change my life forever. After riding their four-wheelers for a while, Dominic's motor failed to start. His friend hooked up a tow rope and was towing his four-wheeler to another friend's house when the rope got wrapped around Dominic's tire and flipped him over, causing a head injury. Chris was the first one to get a call from our neighbor, who told him the police were trying to contact us because Dom had been in an accident. Chris called and told me to call the local police dispatch to figure out what was going on. My heart was racing as I called the number. I listened as the man told me that Dominic had had an accident and was being transported by ambulance to the hospital. I asked if he was OK and was told that they had no additional information, and I was to contact the hospital.

I dropped everything and drove to the ER to find my son. I expected a broken bone, or cuts and stitches, but nothing could have prepared me for what I was about to find out. As I waited to see my son, I called my mother and my family members, who each came to the hospital to wait for an answer with me. We were moved to a waiting area, and finally the on-call neurosurgeon came in to discuss Dom's condition. He told us that Dom had suffered a severe brain injury from the accident, which caused his brain to shift and swell. Hearing this news, our hearts sank. I heard the doctor and the devastating words, but somehow, in my mind, I thought he would still be all right. When I was finally allowed to see him, they took me to a room in the ER where he was. Dominic was lying in a hospital bed, hooked up to several machines, seemingly just sleeping. Once I was with him, I refused to leave his side. I followed alongside his bed as he was transferred to the ICU. I have so many vivid memories from that day that will forever be etched in my mind. I remember racing down the hall with Dom, passing by the same waiting room I had been in earlier and noticing it was now overflowing with even more family and friends. After we were settled in the ICU, I was able to call Chris. Knowing he had a long drive home, I tried to keep the severity of the situation hidden from him. I merely told him that he needed to come home right away. I later found out that my family had been in touch with him as he was making his way home and had filled him in on Dom's condition. Chris walked into the ICU around midnight, and I could see the tension in his face as he assessed the room and saw Dominic. I explained all that I knew up to that moment and what the doctors had told us.

News of Dominic's accident spread throughout our small community, and for the next two days, there were hundreds of friends and family in and out of the hospital. The staff was compassionate enough to allow people back to see Dom in small groups. We heard from many people who had gathered to pray the rosary for Dominic, and a large group of his friends and classmates got together at our local park to release sky lanterns and make posters. Dom's classmates came up with the saying *DO IT FOR DOM,* which quickly spread through town. It was basketball season, and our school had a game against a local rivalry. Both teams, as well as a huge student crowd, wore white shirts to the game with the saying *DO IT FOR DOM* on the back. The outpouring of love that so many people had for our son was amazing. We clung to hope and prayed that things would improve. All the while, Dom's condition remained unchanged.

On Saturday, we were asked to gather in a small private room. A few minutes later, a lady from Mid-America Transplant, our area organ procurement organization (OPO) entered the room. She introduced herself as Jonette and began talking to us about the possibility of organ donation. Chris and I were shocked and very much in denial at that time. We were still praying for our miracle, and this lady was sitting in front of us talking about things that we were unprepared to hear. Our first meeting with Jonette was not at all pleasant or civil. Later that evening, after the doctors had the results of many more tests, we were told that Dominic's condition was worsening. He was scheduled for a test the next morning to check for brain activity. Our worst fears were coming to fruition. It seemed that the doctors had little hope that Dominic would recover from his accident. We were given some time to absorb the news, and eventually, we were again taken to a small private room where Jonette joined us. She was very compassionate, as she once again discussed the possibility of donation. Dominic was 17 years old and not a registered donor. Neither was Chris or myself. We knew absolutely nothing about Mid-America Transplant, nor about organ, eye, and tissue donation. After speaking with Jonette, and knowing our son and how giving he was, the answer, although difficult, was one of the easiest decisions we had to make that weekend. On Sunday morning, February 23rd, 2014, my son, Dominic… my baby, my whole world, was declared brain dead. Everyone in our family was shattered by the news. We spent the day by Dom's side, trying to soak in everything we could before he had to leave us.

Jonette returned Sunday in the early evening, and we began answering questions about Dominic's medical social history. I remember being so exhausted and completely overwhelmed. I had not slept in the three days that Dom was in the hospital. The questions were extensive, and Jonette was very patient with us as we asked our own questions too. I had to know everything that was going to happen to my son. To this day, I do not know how we managed to get through those three days, and to make the decisions that we had to make. We listened as Jonette explained that Dominic would be transferred two hours north to Mid-America Transplant in St. Louis, where they would begin testing and start the process of finding compatible recipients. We stayed with Dom until the transport arrived to take him to St. Louis. Chris and I gathered all of Dominic's things and started our walk down the long hallway toward the exit. I vividly remember thinking this can't be real, that this couldn't be happening to my son, to our family, to us. We were leaving the hospital without Dominic. How in the world could anything ever be right again in our lives after this? We, along with almost our entire community, had been praying for three days for a miracle. A miracle was about to happen, but not for Dominic as we had prayed for. It was about to happen for "The Lucky Five."

Chris and I left the hospital believing we had done what Dominic would have wanted. We were told he would potentially be able to save eight lives through his organ donation. As the days passed, and my mind realized that this nightmare was actually real, I began to second guess our decisions. I worried that we made the wrong choices. My mind kept circling through all the events of those three long hospital days. I somehow created several "what if" scenarios. What if he had been able to recover with time? What if the doctors missed something? What if I had demanded that he be transferred to a different hospital? What if choosing to donate caused his death? Did I make the right decision? I knew all the answers to my questions. We knew the results, and we knew Dominic was gone. We knew donation was the answer, but my mind and my heart were just not able to accept any of it. I went through many days of doubt.

About one month after we lost Dom, I went to the mailbox and saw that we had received a letter from Mid-America Transplant. My heart was practically beating out of my chest, and I trembled as I tried to open the envelope. With tears smearing the page, I read about the five lives that were changed because of Dominic's generous gift of life. Suddenly, my days of doubt and second guessing the decisions we had made ended. My son was a hero to five individuals. He was their miracle. They were "The Lucky Five." The letter stated: "Dominic's heart now beats for a 27-year-old man from Ohio. The recipient of Dominic's liver is a 7-year-old girl from Colorado. Dominic's lungs were given to a 43-year-old man from Missouri. Dominic's left kidney and pancreas were gifted to a 31-year-old man from Missouri. The recipient of Dominic's right kidney is a 40-year-old woman from Missouri."

In March of 2014, we received a card, via Mid-America Transplant, from a lady named Sandy, who said she was the aunt of the man who had received Dominic's lungs: Scott. She wanted to thank us for Dom's gift on behalf of her sister, Scott's mother, who had passed away. It was a very short, sweet letter, and knowing they were grateful gave us comfort. In August, we received another letter, only this time it was from Scott himself. I cried as I read about his life and children. I could really feel the gratitude come through the pages. Scott's letter inspired me, and I immediately sat down and wrote my very first letter to Dominic's recipients. Tears ran down my face through the entire process. I wanted to share who my son was with those *lucky five* individuals. I wanted them to understand, and to know how loved Dom was and still is. It was so hard to convey those feelings on paper. I shared about Dominic's life: his interests, hobbies, passions, his personality and his drive. It was my hope that the recipients would appreciate knowing who their hero was. We enclosed some pictures of Dominic with that first letter, as well as car decals we had made with the saying *DO IT FOR DOM*. That special saying had turned into our family motto. About two months later, we received a letter from Jacob, Dominic's heart recipient. We again got the chance to see how Dom's gift had helped another person get a second chance at life. Jacob told us that he was able to be there for the birth of his niece and travel to his best friend's wedding because of Dominic. When Christmas came that year, I decided to buy an ornament for each of Dominic's recipients and to write a letter about him and how the ornament pertained to him or his life. This turned into a yearly tradition, and so far, we have sent eight different ornaments, ranging from sports to video games and music. Each letter gives a glimpse into Dom's life and also lets me stroll down memory lane when I write them.

In March of 2015, we attended a candlelight vigil/donor tribute ceremony in St. Louis through Mid-America Transplant, and while we were there, I was handed an envelope. I quickly opened it to find a letter from the family of Alondra, the 7-year-old girl who had received Dom's liver. Can you imagine being so young and receiving a life-saving transplant? They included a picture of the sweet girl, and she looked absolutely beautiful in a blue dress, with a white bow in her hair. I kept staring at her little angelic face, crying both happy and sad tears. Dominic had such a love for his younger cousins, and I know he would have been so proud to know that he had helped this little girl. I mourned the loss of my son so much, but through the letters I had been receiving, I was also able to rejoice in the recipients' lives, and in how Dom's legacy was living on. 2015 was a big year for our family, as we had the honor and privilege of meeting Jacob, Dominic's heart recipient. Jacob and I met each other by chance through a mutual Facebook group in January, and in June, he traveled from Ohio to Missouri to meet me, Chris, and our family. He and his mother drove over nine hours, and they brought a stethoscope so we could once again hear our son's heartbeat.

I did a lot of research as we became more involved with donation. One day, I came across a website called The Transplant Games of America. I learned that these games, held every two years, are a celebration of life for recipients, donors, and living donors. Their mission is to increase awareness of the life-restoring importance of organ, cornea, bone marrow, and tissue donation by showcasing the lives of the athlete-recipients, the living donors, and the lasting legacy of their donors. After reading about how special these games were, I immediately told Chris that we were going to the next event, to be held in 2016. I contacted Mid-America Transplant and joined *Team United St. Louis*. In November of 2015, I attended a team welcome meeting at Mid-America Transplant to participate as a donor family in the Transplant Games. At the time, Chris was still going through a lot of anger over losing Dominic. He had no interest at all in going to the games, especially to watch recipients celebrate life at the expense of Dom. He did not want anything to do with the games and did not accompany me to the meeting. I was sitting in the meeting room, waiting for things to start, when I noticed the staff of Mid-America frantically walking in and out of the room. I didn't understand what all the commotion was about. A short while later,

I was approached by a lady from Mid-America Transplant who said, "Dominic's lung recipient is here. We didn't know you'd both be here today. Would you like to meet him?" Of course, I said yes. They took me to a small back room, and moments later, Scott, Dom's double lung recipient, and his wife, Michelle, walked in. I was shaking as we were introduced to each other. With tears in my eyes, I hugged Scott. I could feel him take a deep breath as we embraced. That deep breath was only possible because of my son Dominic. I listened as I was told the story of Scott's illness, about how simple tasks like getting up to walk across the room had been difficult. Michelle told me that after Scott woke up from his transplant surgery, he said he hadn't felt that good since he was a teenager. The story amazed me, especially since they had no information on Dominic, including his age, yet Scott had felt like a teenager again. That was my son! I left that meeting and called Chris right away, then several family members, and told them of my chance meeting with Scott.

Years later, we talked with Scott about that surprise meeting. He told me he knew there was a chance that I would be at the meeting, and he was very anxious about meeting me. A few days prior to the meeting, Scott was told by the staff at Mid-America that I wasn't able to attend. He told me he was shocked and saddened to hear how young Dominic was when he received my first letter, but when he walked into the small backroom that day, a sense of calm descended on him as I had welcomed him so warmly. He went on to tell us that Dominic has a wonderful large family and it has been a blessing to him. Scott also told us he's amazed at how we all work hand in hand to bring so much awareness to donation.

In July of 2016, Chris and I, as well as several of my family members, attended the Transplant Games of America, which were held in Cleveland, Ohio. Chris was still against going and made that very apparent while we were driving to Cleveland. Once we arrived, I asked him to come with me to the convention center to get our registration packet. He grudgingly obliged. Within five minutes of walking through the door, a gentleman came up to us because he noticed from our badges that we were a donor family and dropped to his knees right in front of us to thank us. After he left, Chris turned to me and said, "I'm sorry, you were right. We are coming to these games from now on." That one gesture of gratitude from a stranger was enough to change Chris's heart, as well as open his eyes to the fact that even in our loss, we could rejoice in the gifts that Dominic had given, rejoice knowing that there was a light in the darkness. Those first Transplant Games will always hold a special place in our hearts.

Also in attendance at these games were Jacob, Dominic's heart recipient, and Scott, Dom's double-lung recipient and his wife, Michelle, and their children, Alexia and Jack.. We, once again, got to see Dominic play his favorite sport, basketball, only now it was through Scott. Another beautiful experience we had was the privilege of placing a medal around Jacob's neck after his team won first place in trivia. We were among hundreds of donor families from across the country and the world, watching the amazing power of donation through the recipients as they competed not only for themselves, but for their donors as well. The feelings were indescribable. I was extremely thankful that we had the opportunity to be there, and also blessed that the games helped Chris find his peace. The Transplant Games of America healed Chris, bringing him back from a very dark place and strengthening his desire to spread the word about donation. He has since gone through training with Mid-America Transplant and is now a volunteer who speaks at local schools to help educate children on the importance of registering as an organ, eye, and tissue donor.

As we navigate life without Dominic, we have met with many struggles and challenges. Chris and I found a new purpose in life, which is to remember and honor Dominic in everything we do. We continue to raise awareness and help educate our community, and surrounding areas, about donation. We continue to keep in contact with Jacob and Scott, as well as send letters to all of Dom's recipients. In October of 2016, I received a Facebook message from Dominic's kidney recipient, Charlene, who told us that because of Dominic she was able to live again. She wanted to let us know that she received every letter and ornament we had sent, and she was hoping for the chance to get to know us and our family. Charlene went on to say that her dream was to get married, and because of Dominic, she was about to fulfill that dream. She invited us to her wedding that was to be held that month – in November. I was honored she asked us to attend but unsure about going. I didn't want to take anything away from her special day, plus I knew it would be a very emotional time for me. Chris was going to be out of town for work the weekend of her wedding, and I was nervous about attempting another recipient meeting alone. I kept telling myself I shouldn't go, but as the days went by, I began to change my mind. Something in my heart kept telling me that I had to be there. I never told Charlene I was coming. On the day of her wedding, I sat with my friend and watched Charlene marry her husband, Neil. No one knew who we were, but somehow, I felt as though I belonged there. At the end of the ceremony, we stood in line to greet the couple as we left. I nervously asked my friend to go ahead of me. She congratulated Charlene and Neil and then turned to introduce me to them as Dominic's mom. I held my breath as I gauged their reaction, fearful that I was wrong for showing up unannounced. I could see that Charlene was shocked, but I could also see the gratitude in her eyes. She hugged me, thanked me profusely for coming, and then introduced me to her husband, who was frantically trying to get something from his back pocket. I had no idea what he was doing, until he pulled out his wallet and opened it up to a picture of my sweet boy, Dominic. He told me that he had carried Dom with him since the day they received the pictures with my first letter. We hugged, and with tears streaming down my face, I knew I had made the right decision to come. Another circle of Dom's amazing life had been completed after I met his kidney recipient.

When we are able to see the huge ripple effect of Dominic's donation through his recipients, it really put things into perspective. Dom not only saved their lives, but he also made a difference in the countless lives that each one of these recipient's touch. Chris and I have spoken with many donor families and recipients, and with each conversation, we try to encourage them to reach out. The communication and connections we've made with Dom's recipients has helped us tremendously on our journey. I could have never dreamed that out of the "Lucky Five," we would have been blessed to hear from four recipients and meet three in person. We still have hope that someday we will meet those last two lucky people.

Another dream, or bucket-list item, of ours was to have Dominic represented as a donor on the Donate Life Float in the Rose Parade. In late 2019, we were surprised and overjoyed when we found out that Mid-America Transplant had selected Dominic to be honored with a floragraph in the 2020 New Year's Day parade. His portrait was created with floral and organic materials and displayed on the float during the parade. The theme for the float that year was "Light in the Darkness," and we felt there couldn't have been a better fitting theme, since we were constantly being shown the light in the darkness by Dom's recipients. We held a floragraph "reveal party" in our hometown and invited family and friends, along with three of Dominic's recipients. It was a very powerful event, where Chris and I, as well as Jacob, Scott, and Charlene, were able to put the finishing touches on Dom's portrait before it was sent to California to adorn the float. On New Year's Day, January 1st, 2020, we sat on the sidelines in Pasadena, California, watching the Rose Parade and cheering as the Donate Life Float passed. Our hearts exploded with joy and pride at Dom having become a part of the Rose Bowl.

Chris and I, as well as Jonette, Scott, Michelle, Alexia, and Jack, are now registered donors because of Dom's accident. We learned so much about a very important topic, one that far too many people know little about. We were among those uneducated people prior to that weekend in February of 2014. Now, we spread the message about the importance of registering as a donor, as well as the importance of discussing your decisions with your family and loved ones. Although we know we made the right decision for our son, if we had had the discussion with him earlier, we would have never had to question our decision. We are proud of the huge impact Dom has made on so many people in our community. We have received so much support and encouragement for continuing our mission to educate and create awareness for organ, eye, and tissue donation.

Dominic's high school football and baseball coach, Jim May approached us, asking if he could dedicate a football game to Dominic and help us spread the word about donation. In September of 2014, we were invited to a home football game and asked to be honorary captains. Chris and I showed up on the field and saw "DOM" on the 35-yard-line at each end of the football field. Coach May had spent the day painting Dom's name on both ends of the field to honor and remember our son, whose jersey number was 35. That special game sparked a new tradition at Scott City High School. They now have football, baseball, and softball "green out games" to honor Dominic, and to bring awareness to the need for registered donors. The high school teams purchased green uniforms and jerseys for each sport, so they could be worn at these special games. We also design and sell green T-shirts with *Dominic* and *Donate Life* on them, and the proceeds benefit Mid-America Transplant. Our school colors are blue and gold, but once we started the "green out games," you would think green was the color, as almost every student and teacher wears a green *Dom* shirt.

Chris and I have worked tirelessly to honor and remember Dom by raising donor awareness in Southeast Missouri and by encouraging others to register as organ, eye, and tissue donors. Several businesses in the Scott City area have also helped play a part in our efforts by displaying blue-and-green ribbons throughout the month of April, which is National Donate Life Month. Through conversations with our local DMV, we learned that our area donor registration has increased 200 percent since Dominic's accident. Chris and I are extremely proud to be known in our area as Dom's mom and dad, and we are truly humbled by the continued support of our family, friends, and community. The tragic loss of Dominic has changed our lives forever, but because of his selfless gift, his legacy continues on. Because of organ donation, we have a new extended family through Dom's recipients – those *lucky five*. We choose to honor Dominic every day and the gifts he gave. Our hope is to always inspire others to look for the light in the darkness, and, of course, *DO IT FOR DOM*.

About Sara

Sara (Hooper) Snider lives in Scott City, Missouri, with her husband, Chris Snider. She is the proud mother of her late son Dominic Hooper, and stepmother to Amanda and Drake Snider, who reside in Taylorsville, Kentucky. Sara is a customer service manager for an industrial tooling distributor. Sara enjoys helping others, laughing, and making memories with family and friends. She is a dedicated volunteer for Mid-America Transplant and Team United.

Family is everything to Sara. She is the youngest of four girls who were raised by her mother, Charlotte, and longtime family friend, Joan. She has a very close-knit family and enjoys spending time with her older sisters, Christine, Becky, and Cheryl, and all of her beloved nieces, nephews, and great nieces, as well as her mother-in-law, Barbara.

Sara and Chris are passionate about educating and spreading awareness for organ donation. In addition to establishing the "Green Out" games at their local high school, they have also helped kickstart games at the collegiate level with several local colleges. Their efforts extended to reach people on a state level when they met with the Missouri State Representative, Jamie Burger, and testified in a committee hearing to designate April 16th as "Missouri Donate Life Day." The bill, which has passed through the House, encourages the citizens of Missouri to participate in appropriate activities and events to increase public awareness of the need for organ donation and organ donors.

Sara and Chris are continuously inspired by donors and recipients. They consider themselves extremely honored to have an even larger family through the lives that their son Dominic has saved and look forward to enjoying many more years with them. Chris and Sara are extremely thankful for their huge support system through family, friends, church and community In the words of Pablo Picasso: "The meaning of life is to find your gift. The purpose of life is to give it away." May the gifts that Dominic has selflessly given to five others inspire you to give your gifts as well. DO IT FOR DOM.

Dominic Hooper, 2014

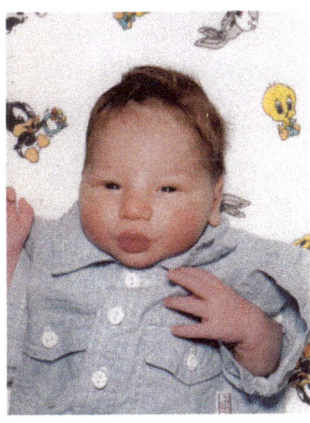

*Dominic Michael Hooper—
hospital, June 28, 1996.*

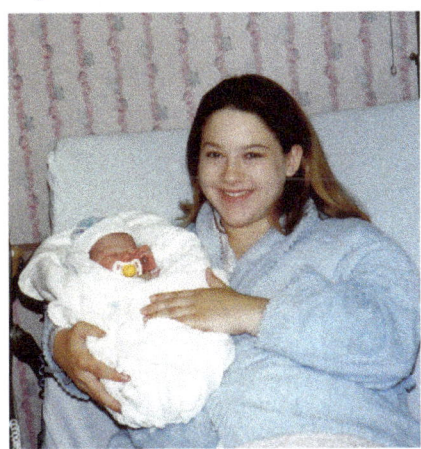

Sara and Dominic—June 28, 1996.

Dominic walking Sara down the aisle, March 27, 2010.

DOM on football field with 2015 football team.

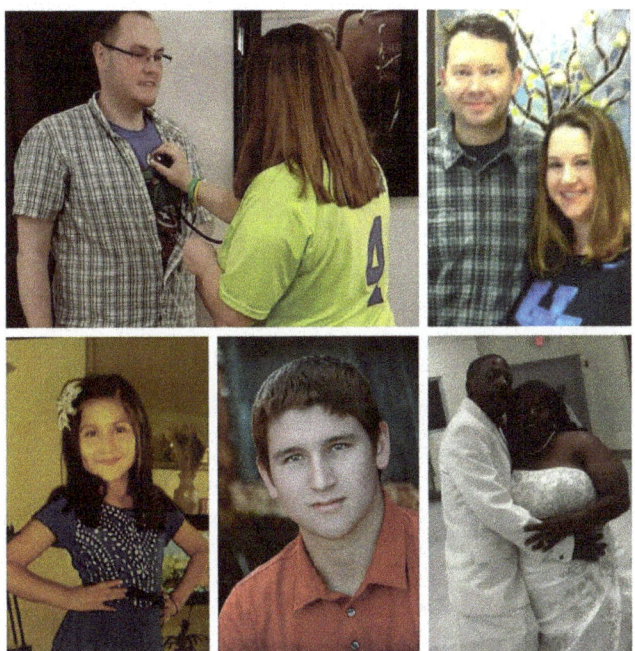

Four of the lucky five.

Our first Green Out game profits donated to Mid-America Transplant in honor of Dominic. Pictured, Coach Jim May, Jonette Strothcamp, Sara, and Chris.

Chris and Sara at 2016 Transplant Games of America, Cleveland, Ohio.

Floragraph reveal party. Pictured Scott Holden (double lung recipient), Jacob Feicht (heart recipient) and his son Carter Lee Dominic Feight, Charlene Hughes (kidney recipient), Sara, Chris, and Jonette Strothcamp.

Donate Life Float 2020 Rose Bowl Parade, Pasadena California.

Dominic Hooper—Football, 2014.

Dominic Hooper—Basketball, 2014.

Dominic Hooper— Baseball, 2014.

In memory of Dominic Hooper
1996 – 2014.

Silver Linings

By Patti DiSanto

I don't tell the story of my son's transplant and recovery, or my side story of personal survival, very often. My husband, Victor, is the public speaker and he's great at it. He talks about organ donation at high schools, hospitals, and donation/transplantation events. He can share a condensed yet captivating version of our family's journey in ten minutes or less, and really get the point across about the importance of registering to be an organ donor. His delivery of how a young boy from their community, who was healthy and active, suddenly needed a transplant to survive is very powerful.

I, on the other hand, am more of a spontaneous storyteller, sharing snippets of our story with those facing similar challenges to help them feel comforted, less alone, and more aware of useful resources. Victor and I are both passionate about raising awareness and helping others touched by donation and transplantation. We were not expecting this journey, nor were we prepared for it. We made it through mostly on autopilot, and with the help of our family, friends, community, and medical professionals – our village. We're now part of a larger village, finding ways to do for others what was done for us.

Our story does not define us, but it's a part of us and it unites us. It has a lot of twists and turns, and it's not over. It's not easy to give the condensed version, but the bottom line is the same: A hero registered to be an organ donor and saved our son Joe's life and saved our family.

My lens is that of a mom and caregiver. I've always played a helper role; I am a people pleaser, but that role quickly expanded in ways I never imagined when Joe was diagnosed with dilated cardiomyopathy in 2005. It was completely unexpected and life-altering. It had a profound effect on our entire family and changed the course of our lives in many ways.

I relive bits and pieces of our journey all the time, triggered by obvious and not-so-obvious reminders of scary and overwhelming moments, miraculous and triumphant moments, and everything in between. Scenes from the past play in my head in vivid detail, usually causing me to shake my head in disbelief that it actually happened and that I somehow avoided having a complete mental breakdown. I credit that to my husband, who never left my side, my amazing family and friends, the medical miracle workers, and our community who rallied around us in so many ways, big and small. A silver lining for sure.

Joe was an active, healthy kid. He was into sports from the minute he could grip a ball and bounce it off the floor and walls. Legos and trucks collected dust in our house; he was all about balls of every size, color, and type. He has played football, basketball, and baseball since he was five. Victor coached many of his teams, and their free time, friendships, and interests revolved around sports. Joe's older sister, Laura, was into Girl Scouts, dance, and shopping; I was her Girl Scout leader and shopping partner. We loved spending time together with friends and family, playing games, watching TV, listening to music, and finding humor in just about anything. We were leading the typical crazy life of two working parents with two busy kids.

When Joe was in fifth grade, I brought him to the pediatrician to get a form signed for a weeklong basketball sleepaway camp. His doctor performed the routine checkup and noticed his heart rate was faster than normal. He asked if Joe had recently been sick, which he hadn't. After lab work ruled out any infection, he referred us to a pediatric cardiologist to make sure everything was okay. I wasn't concerned. Joe didn't show any symptoms; he was also super active, and it just didn't occur to me that something serious could be wrong. Looking back, it's surprising that I wasn't concerned. I'm a ridiculous worrier, the ultimate overprotective mom.

The pediatric cardiologist did an echocardiogram and knew instantly why Joe's heart rate was so fast. He drew us a picture of Joe's heart, showing that it was severely enlarged, and then he explained the details of dilated cardiomyopathy. Joe's version was idiopathic, meaning he wasn't born with a heart defect; it had happened for an unknown reason, likely a virus that had attacked his heart. He said one third of kids with cardiomyopathy get better with medication, one third stay the same, and one third get worse and might eventually need a heart transplant. Joe would be put on a cocktail of medications and monitored weekly at their office at Robert Wood Johnson University Hospital (RWJ). He would have to stop playing all sports, except golf or bowling.

Victor's first response was to ask if Joe could get a heart transplant right away. The doctor said he could only be listed for a transplant if he was so sick that there were no other options. The good news was that Joe had no symptoms; his heart was compensating. Despite Victor's question, I barely registered the word "transplant." Always optimistic, I went down the "one third get better" path immediately. I had zero knowledge about organ donation, other than I had checked "Yes" to organ donation when I got my driver's license at seventeen, but that was a no-brainer for me. I didn't correlate that to someone getting a transplant. It was just a logical "you can't take it with you" choice.

Joe's diagnosis turned our lives upside down. He was playing baseball, about to start summer football, and looking forward to a week of basketball camp. It was a gut punch to all of us, especially Joe. His friendships and activities were intertwined with sports. It was a rough summer. I enrolled him in computer camp and golf camp. I mentioned drama camp and he cried, and I cried for him. We were all emotionally fragile and trying to deal with Joe's diagnosis in our own ways. There was arguing, yelling, and crying for many different reasons. We were a tight family, but we were in rocky waters. I was slipping with my people-pleaser role at times – and with my own family, no less! There was no playbook for this.

We weaved our way through the obstacle course of our "new normal" that summer. We took Joe to see his cardiologist weekly so they could administer heart meds and monitor his vitals. The entire medical team was incredibly compassionate and gave us a true feeling of security when we were there. Word of Joe's situation began to spread among his friends, their parents, and our family and friends, but he wasn't feeling or showing any symptoms, so he looked "normal" on the outside. There was hope, at least in my mind, that the heart meds would do the trick.

Joe was a mellow, somewhat introverted kid, not one to share his feelings, and his diagnosis didn't change this. He stayed connected to friends, keeping score for his baseball team and scheduling sleepovers. As the summer came to a close, we met with school leadership and nurses to make staff aware of his medical condition and create a plan for the school year. Joe was eleven and starting sixth grade, and Laura was fifteen and starting tenth grade. We fell into a groove, managed to relax a little, laugh a little, and let our guard down a little.

My list of fears was expanding, but I kept them to myself. Anytime I heard a siren when I wasn't with Joe, I worried it was for him. Most nights I tiptoed into his room while he was sleeping to make sure he was still breathing. I think I was afraid to share my true feelings with others, as if voicing them would make my worst fears a reality. I attempted to keep the family unit happy and positive, but there were challenges. I wasn't winning any mom awards; my fears and inability to fix everything turned into some breakdowns where I lost control, screamed like a wild woman, and took my anxiety out on my favorite people.

Victor and Joe went to a New Jersey Nets game at the Meadowlands in early winter. It was a super cold night; they were bundled up and waiting outside for the arena doors to open. Once inside, they were making their way through the warm, crowded concourse when Joe started to feel dizzy. As Victor steered him toward a bench to sit down, a woman approached them to see if Joe was okay. She said she was a nurse and noticed Joe looked like he was about to pass out. Victor explained Joe's medical condition, and this nurse, who seemed to appear out of thin air, shared that she was a heart transplant coordinator at the Children's Hospital of New York Presbyterian (CHONY). She was extremely familiar with cardiomyopathy, and even knew the pediatric cardiologist treating Joe. She explained that Joe likely felt faint because his compromised heart was working extra hard to adjust from the cold outdoors to the warm temperature of the arena.

The next day, I got a call from this nurse. She introduced herself and said she was calling to see how Joe was doing. What a sweetheart! Not to mention the crazy coincidence that a pediatric cardiology nurse saw Joe in a crowded concourse on the brink of passing out. This is one of many examples of nurses who went above and beyond for us; they don't get nearly enough credit.

Joe's cardiologist had already told us that if Joe ever needed a transplant, he would go to CHONY because there weren't any pediatric heart transplant programs in New Jersey. After the incident at the Nets game, Joe's wise doctor decided he should have a heart catheterization at CHONY for two reasons. The first was to have another view of Joe's heart function to confirm his treatment or make any changes. The other reason was to ensure our first visit there was not an emergency situation. At this appointment, the doctors confirmed his heart was very enlarged but was compensating well. No changes to his treatment were required.

Two months later, one night after dinner, Joe began to act strange, almost delirious. I couldn't understand what he was saying. I was scared and immediately called his cardiologist and spoke with the doctor on-call. It was my first encounter with this particular doctor; he was comforting and in control. He asked to speak with Joe and had him answer some questions. He said Joe sounded okay, but I didn't sound okay. He told us to take Joe to RWJ's emergency room to have him checked out to be on the safe side. Victor and I rushed Joe over there.

By the time we arrived, Joe was acting more like himself. We were more relaxed and cracking jokes as Victor played with the medical equipment in the room while waiting for the doctor. They checked Joe's vitals, took a chest X-ray, and diagnosed him with a slight case of pneumonia. I spoke with the cardiologist by phone; he wanted to admit Joe and start IV antibiotics. The doctor repeated that it was "just to be on the safe side" because Joe was a heart patient. Victor and I followed Joe to the inpatient floor, where the nurse got him settled and showed us a lounge chair where one of us could sleep. Victor went home to be with Laura, and Joe and I were asleep shortly after.

A few hours later, Joe called out to me saying his stomach hurt. I ran over to the bed to ask where it hurt, and he didn't answer. I realized he wasn't responding and quickly hit the nurse's call button. The nurse came in, and within seconds, there was a code blue and tons of people streaming into his room, shouting commands. Joe had gone into cardiac arrest. The medical team was performing chest compressions and using paddles, and I saw a giant needle in his leg. I was frozen, afraid to look or listen to what was happening, and then I started to pace.

I stepped outside his room and frantically called home – and got the answering machine! Not surprising since it was around 3:00 am. I called again. Laura answered and woke Victor. I told him to get back to the hospital as fast as he could. He asked what was going on, but I just repeated that he had to get back right away.

Then I heard a doctor say, "Call clergy for the mom!" I knew that wasn't good. I kept pacing outside Joe's door while the chest compressions continued. A clergywoman approached me and tried to comfort me. She was tall with red hair, but I don't remember a word she said. Victor arrived, out of breath; he took in the visual of Joe's room packed with doctors and nurses and quickly registered that Joe was in serious trouble.

They finally got Joe's heart going and wheeled him away to the ICU. He had IVs everywhere and he was unconscious, with nurses and doctors hovering over him. The cardiologist who I had spoken with by phone rushed toward us and wrapped me in a big hug, shaking his head in disbelief. He took us into a room where the head ICU doctor joined us. She said they had managed to stabilize him, but he was in grave condition. An ambulance with cardiac specialists from CHONY was on its way. The CHONY team would come up with a plan, but it was clear that Joe needed a transplant, and soon. All I could hear was the "wah wah wah wah" voice from a Charlie Brown movie.

My gaze drifted to a whiteboard on the opposite wall with a video sitting on the ledge. There was no TV or VCR in this room, but Laura and Joe's favorite Disney movie, *Mary Poppins*, was sitting on that whiteboard ledge. I was convinced Mary Poppins, our "practically perfect" family heroine, was looking over Joe – and all of us. Shortly after, we were in Joe's ICU room and I was looking at him, utterly terrified. It was dark and rainy outside his window, but then a huge rainbow appeared. I immediately had a feeling that my dad was watching over him. Another sign, a flash of hope.

We were told to go home, pack clothes, get things in order, and head to CHONY. We were in shock and half numb. We went back to Joe's original room, empty now without the bed, to get my things. The nurse who was caring for Joe when he was admitted was sitting on the floor, in tears, clearly shaken up over the unexpected scene that had just played out. She collected herself and wished us well. We reconnected with this nurse more than ten years later. She didn't know that Joe had survived; it was a moving reunion.

We spent the next three months in CHONY's cardiac ICU (CICU). Victor and I literally lived in his room, sleeping on a window seat with hospital blankets, freezing our buns off every day in the climate-controlled medical icebox. His room overlooked a busy city street with people hustling back and forth, day and night. Yankee Stadium was off in the distance; we could see the stadium lights for home games, and there were many. Another comfort in the midst of fear, beeping machines, tons of medical people, and an unconscious Joe.

We were told Joe needed a heart transplant, but since he was in such serious condition, he would first need to undergo surgery to connect him to a heart machine called a BiVAD. His heart could no longer do its job. Within hours of arriving, Joe underwent a twelve-hour surgery. He was between life and death, being kept alive by the BiVAD, a ventilator, and a host of other machines, IVs, and tubes. His organs were shutting down, he needed countless transfusions, and he was incredibly frail from the BiVAD surgery. He was also in a medically induced coma so his body could slowly recover and eventually prepare for transplant surgery. That BiVAD was the largest machine in the room, the size of a stove, with tubes that connected into Joe's body. The machine was actually meant for adults, but his surgeon thought that Joe was on the edge of being adult sized, so it would be the best choice for him. He was also connected to a dialysis machine; his kidneys were failing, he was bleeding uncontrollably, and one lung had collapsed. They officially listed him for a transplant, but with nearly unmatchable criteria because he wouldn't survive another surgery at this point.

Joe's heart surgeon was brilliant and had an amazing bedside manner. He presented understandable explanations and options for every medical challenge that Joe faced, and he was honest. He told us early on that he was not sure if Joe was going to make it, but he delivered news in a way that made us feel like he was in control and that there was hope. We named him "Jolly Jonny" the day he woke us at 6:00 am to say Joe needed a kidney transplant, along with a heart transplant. He assured us it wasn't a bad thing; because he was already getting a transplant, the same anti-rejection meds would be used, same recovery involved. His positive, confident spin was an anchor we held on to for dear life. And the transplant team, a trio of female superheroes, worked closely with the surgeon to get Joe strong enough for transplant surgery and beyond. They were honest too, yet reassuring and patient with our constant questions.

We encountered so many people every day, from medical professionals to housekeeping to other CICU families. We gave many of them nicknames from TV and movie characters; it was the only way we could keep track. Joe's care was complex, and the doctors weren't always on the same page. His heart was the main attraction, and his surgeon and cardiology superheroes were in charge, but ICU doctors also had a say in his treatment, and specialists had to weigh in too. CHONY is a teaching hospital, so there were always lots of white coats in Joe's room. We had to adjust to the daily, weekly, and monthly rotations of doctors and nurses. They were all our heroes, even the ones with the less-than-stellar bedside manners; they were collectively keeping our son alive. We participated as much as we could during rounds and specialist visits, since we were with him around the clock and could describe what we had observed. We never wanted to leave the room in fear we'd miss talking with one of them – they held the answers. Of course, they didn't have all the answers, and even after the most critical first month, new problems popped up regularly. It was a cycle of one step forward and two steps back.

The nurses who sat outside his fishbowl room were the front line of Joe's care, the glue that held everything together. They were beyond amazing, acting as our translators and our teachers. They kept Joe alive and helped us take care of him and ourselves. They were compassionate and kind, and so skilled with Joe's complex care. His monitor was beeping around the clock the first few weeks; those nurses did not have much down time. Joe went into cardiac arrest more than once and faced other life-threatening complications.

I was so scared that I either paced outside his room or huddled on a couch in the family lounge, playing Sudoku to mentally escape reality. I still have completed Sudoku books with questions and feelings scribbled on many pages. I could hear beeping from beyond and knew it was Joe. It wasn't just the gravity of the situation that scared me. Joe physically looked near death, tubes everywhere, with parts of his chest exposed that I didn't want to see and couldn't unsee. Victor, on the other hand, didn't leave the room. Day and night for the first five weeks, Victor had the TV tuned to a Yankee game or sports show, giving unconscious Joe play-by-play commentary.

Joe was a fighter. As he started to show small signs of improvement, I spent more time in his room. He was still on the ventilator and heavily sedated but could hear us. Victor and I held his hands, and he squeezed back. We talked to him and explained what was going on around him. Family and friends visited regularly, traveling long distances, bringing Laura for visits, and providing food and comfort. Joe turned twelve on the ventilator, and I wouldn't let anyone say happy birthday because I didn't want to scare him if he wasn't lucid enough to know where he was and why.

After six weeks and two (quite scary) failed attempts, his breathing tube was successfully removed. But Joe did not immediately start talking or acting like himself. He hallucinated on and off. He asked about the kids in the room reading books and the people under the bed. Anti-psychotic meds were added to the mix. We were hopeful yet anxious. When would we see the real Joe? There was concern about trauma to his brain because it had taken so long to revive him after his first cardiac arrest at RWJ.

On a positive note, Joe's kidneys came back to life, and the kidney transplant was off the table. The nurses cheered along with us. But there were also setbacks and a host of complications. Changes in medications and treatment occurred regularly. Victor and I made a great team. His strengths were my weaknesses, and vice versa. He handled medical procedures, blood, critical moments, and interesting conversation (a.k.a. sports updates). I handled hygiene, food, questions for doctors, and emotional support. We also argued and melted down, but mostly stuck together like glue, living each day as it came. People would comment on how strong we were, but we just took one step at a time, without thinking beyond our next talk with a doctor or Joe's next milestone. We compartmentalized facts and fears as a survival mechanism; we leaned on the medical professionals and our family and friends.

The focus now was for Joe to regain enough strength to withstand transplant surgery. Doctors and nurses urged him to take steps in the hallway. He was still connected to multiple IVs, oxygen, and the BiVAD. It took a team of nurses and physical therapists, along with us following behind him with a wheelchair, to make this happen. Joe had no energy or motivation to even sit in a chair for more than a few minutes. But those first few steps were miraculous, with everyone clapping around him. He did not enjoy the attention; he was weak, uncomfortable, and heavily medicated. Then the team had a genius idea, and they added a service dog to his therapy. The sweet Labrador walked those labored steps beside Joe and sat by his bed afterwards as Joe would calmly pet him. The dog received most of the attention, taking the pressure off Joe. They even put a Yankees shirt on the dog to match the blankets and posters in Joe's room.

Joe improved just enough that transplant was becoming a possibility. His surgeon got "the call," and they tested Joe's blood for compatibility. We were nervous and excited, yet at the same time, sad beyond words for the family of this potential donor. This was the first of five calls, and we soon learned to assume it wouldn't be a match, so we could avoid the emotional rollercoaster.

In addition to physical and occupational therapy, there was the push for Joe to eat. His already thin body had lost a lot of weight, plus he had no appetite, so this was no easy task. Soup and protein drinks were about all he could tolerate. Jolly Jonny was the only one who wasn't so concerned about this issue; he said Joe was going to eat like nobody's business after transplant, considering the healthy doses of steroids in his anti-rejection regimen (and he was right). He was concerned, however, when Joe had a stroke; blood clots were a side effect of the BiVAD. The first time, his words started to slur, and one side of his face drooped. We called for help and nurses loaded his life-saving equipment onto his bed and wheeled him on a wild ride through the CHONY halls to NYP's emergency room for a CT scan. The strokes and crazy rides to the emergency room played out several times. CT scans revealed brain bleeds that impacted his vision, which explained why he was having trouble seeing the baseball scores on TV.

The strokes were getting progressively worse and more frequent, so his surgeon said it was time for transplant, whether he was ready or not. Another stroke could debilitate him to the extent that he wouldn't be eligible for transplant. Once the decision was made to immediately search for a heart, a match was found less than forty-eight hours later, and Joe was being prepped for transplant. It was the middle of the night, so Victor and I tried to get some sleep in the family lounge. In the early light of day, Joe's surgeon came in with an update. I nearly freaked out – what was he doing here, why wasn't he in the operating room with Joe?! It was a complicated surgery, requiring a team of many to disconnect him from the BiVAD and then connect him to his new heart.

On this same day, Laura was heading home from a cruise with her best friend and her parents, our close friends. This trip was planned before Joe's hospitalization and was a godsend during this traumatizing time for her. My mom had moved into our house to be with Laura. Laura was trying to get through schooldays and adjusting to living with Grandma. They were very close, but Laura had never experienced actually living with her. My mom was an intense woman with a strong personality. Laura was no wallflower, but my mom was in charge, no question. She even taught Laura how to drive. Laura and I talked on the phone daily, and friends and family brought her to visit on weekends. We slept in family lounges or deserted hallways with hospital blankets, catching up on both Laura's and Joe's survival. Victor got a call from Laura while Joe was well into his transplant surgery. He asked her about her trip, the weather, and if she had gotten sunburned. Laura interrupted and asked how Joe was doing. Victor said, "Well, he's actually in surgery right now!" Laura couldn't believe he had rambled on with small talk so long. The stars miraculously aligned so that she was home in time to see Joe after surgery.

After twelve hours in surgery, they wheeled Joe back to CICU. His surgeon was smiling, and the new heart was working. Before this, Joe was pale and gray, but now we couldn't miss his rosy, pink cheeks, giving us hope and joy. We also felt the weight of someone else's sorrow, and we were so thankful for their gift but sad to our core for their loss. It was July 8th, 2006, and because of organ donation and a heroic organ donor, our son Joe was given a second chance at life.

Joe's post-transplant recovery began. Not to minimize the gravity of pediatric heart transplant surgery, but we saw at least eight kids have successful heart transplants while we were there, with a surprisingly quick recovery and discharge. Sadly, we also saw kids who did not make it, and our hearts broke for their parents. We became close with several families; we shared stories and meals, slept on waiting-room floors, and held each other's hands. I expected Joe to sail through recovery like many others. But Joe's path was more complicated. He was on heavy doses of anti-rejection meds and began hallucinating again. He kept trying to get out of bed but was unable to walk because his leg muscles had atrophied even more after the long surgery. I was back to feeling scared. A favorite nurse told us that for every day in the hospital, it would take him two days to recover. She said he was the sickest patient she had ever seen, but that he would improve with time.

Within two weeks, Joe was moved from CICU to the step-down heart floor, where he ate everything in sight, thanks to those steroids. He needed a wheelchair and a lot of assistance to get around, but he was improving every day. The medical team recommended that we admit Joe to a rehab facility for him to re-learn to walk and regain mobility.

The rehab facility was only a half hour from our home. I had a cot in Joe's room and accompanied him to his physical therapy and occupational therapy sessions. Victor stayed with him on weekends while I went home to Laura. Joe was finally becoming himself again – the Joe with the dry sense of humor and silly comments we knew and loved. After six weeks of intense therapy, and a lot of back and forth to CHONY for checkups, Joe was ready to come home. It was a miracle! More than five months had passed since he had first landed in the hospital. While he still needed a wheelchair and outpatient physical therapy, he could walk short distances. We celebrated Joe being home with tacos, his favorite meal.

After receiving his gift of life, Joe went from surviving to living. It was a slow process, with small wins that accumulated over time. We made countless visits back to CHONY to test for rejection. He had some rejection episodes and other health challenges, which resulted in a few hospitalizations and surgeries over the next few years. We visited CICU every time we went back to CHONY, and they were thrilled to see him thriving. He had to see a neurologist for his vision and other issues related to his strokes, but he eventually no longer needed that specialized care. Despite missing a lot of school, Joe did not have to repeat sixth grade. He began seventh grade being tutored at home for a few months until he could walk well enough through the crowded middle school hallways.

Shortly after Joe's transplant, we wrote a letter to his donor family. How do you put this kind of thank you into words? We shared Joe's story, his favorite foods, his interests, his family, and how thankful we all were for the gift that had saved his life. Around this time, our family began volunteering with New Jersey's organ procurement organization, New Jersey Sharing Network (NJSN), to connect with our local donation and transplantation community. This organization was a lifeline and has become our family. We were able to give back, advocate for donation, form lifelong friendships, give support and be supported in times of need. NJSN facilitated our eventual meeting with Joe's donor's mom. It was one of the most moving moments in all our lives. She listened to Joe's heart beating while we all looked on with tears of both sadness and joy. She showed us pictures and hugged us all, saying she could see that her daughter had saved all of us.

NJSN was there for us that day and continues to play an important role in our lives. They provide a way to be involved in the mission and work of donation, without focusing every minute on the details of Joe's transplant. Joe just wanted to be a normal kid again. He remembers very little of what happened in the hospital, but he knew he didn't want his life, our lives, to revolve around his transplant. He wanted to live life, grateful for his gift but not defined by it. He wanted to crack up watching *Seinfeld*, go to Bruce Springsteen concerts and Yankee games, play cards, hang out with friends. He has done all of these things and more. Joe completed high school, attended school proms, graduated college, and entered the working world.

Part of our outreach and involvement led us to the Transplant Games, a weeklong, Olympic-style competitive event that is held in a different city every two years for transplant recipients, living donors, donor families, and supporters. Beginning in 2008, Joe competed as a member of Team Liberty and won medals at both the U.S. and World

Transplant Games in ball throw, bowling, golf, bocce, basketball, 5K, and more. We traveled as a family to Pittsburgh, Madison, Grand Rapids, Houston, Cleveland, Salt Lake City, Australia, and Spain. These amazing Transplant Games are so much more than winning medals, although Joe can throw a ball ridiculously far – he always loved throwing balls! Joining the Team Liberty family has allowed us to meet people in the transplant and donation community from all over the world, and we've made lifelong friends who enrich our lives to this day. It was life-changing for all of us and a huge silver lining!

Our family remains deeply committed to the donation and transplantation community. I've since become a Team Liberty manager, and Laura is the treasurer. We truly find joy in introducing new people to the Transplant Games. Victor served on the NJSN board for six years, and he chairs their 5K race. He continues to speak to thousands of students every year about organ donation. Team Liberty and NJSN partner on many events and programs; I love working with these organizations to connect people to support one another.

Joe and Laura are both living on their own now, working and enjoying life. Joe and his fiancée, Kacie, live in North Carolina and will be married in June. Laura lives in Cleveland and will be married in September. We're still a very close family even though we live in different states. We're closer because of our story, another silver lining.

What helped me get through my part of this story? I have never been so scared in my entire life, but between the fabulous people in my village and the silver linings that appeared just when we needed them, I got through it and did my best to help my family get through it. I learned so much along the way. I learned to live by the cliché "Don't sweat the small stuff"; it doesn't matter if the house is a mess or if there are dishes in the sink. It's liberating to let go, be spontaneous, and not overthink the minutiae. Accepting help from others is also something I learned to embrace. People want to help and it's okay to admit you need it. This experience taught me to be careful about judging others and instead to be kind by default; we don't know what they may be facing. I also realized that hydration and nutrition are basic needs for a reason, and I needed fuel to stay alert, whether I was hungry or not. I was reminded that laughter really is the best medicine. It's part of our family fabric, and it helps even when you're in the thick of something scary. My journey showed me that silver linings are everywhere – you just need to grab them. And most importantly, I learned to talk about the importance of organ donation and to ask people to register to be an organ donor. It truly saves lives.

About Patti

Patti DiSanto and her husband, Victor, are empty nesters, living and working in New Jersey. Patti works for a major insurance company in risk engineering strategy and operations. Victor is a partner in a commercial real estate appraisal firm. They enjoy spending time together at Yankee games, listening to music, going for walks, playing cards, and gathering around the firepit with friends and family. They especially love their time with Joe and Laura, in person and virtually. Because of organ donation, they have many milestones to look forward to in 2023, including both Joe's and Laura's weddings, Bruce Springsteen concerts, and holidays. And they are looking forward to the 2024 Transplant Games!

When Patti isn't working at her day job, she is finding silver linings everywhere and helping others find theirs. She is a Team Liberty manager, and Laura is Team Liberty's treasurer, webmaster, and T-shirt designer. Laura and Patti are Team Liberty's dynamic duo at the Transplant Games, cheering on team members and making sure their experience is the best it can be.

Patti received the Transplant Game of America's (TGA) Team Manager of the Year award in 2016 and 2022, a testament to her dedication to her team members as well as to other TGA managers. Patti was a Family Advisory Council member at NYP-CHONY for eight years, with the goal of helping other families faced with hospitalization and complex care. She has since taken on a similar role closer to home at RWJ-Barnabas Health Somerset on the Patient and Family Advisory Council, continuing her goal of helping patients and family navigate care.

She remains beyond grateful to Natalie, Joe's organ donor, and Natalie's mom, who had had the conversation with her daughter about registering to be an organ donor.

You can connect with Patti at teamliberty.patti@gmail.com.

About Joe

Joe is turning 29 in 2023 and lives in North Carolina. It's been almost seventeen years since his heart transplant! He is living life to the fullest, thanks to the selfless act of his organ donor and the multitude of medical miracle workers who had a part in his care. Joe works in finance and enjoys spending time in the outdoors with his fiancée, Kacie, and with their adorable pets and their friends. Joe and Kacie will be married in June, a wonderful milestone that would not have been possible without the ultimate generosity of a young woman named Natalie, who registered to be an organ donor.

Joe enjoys competing in the U.S. and World Transplant Games. The Team Liberty family opened their arms to the DiSanto family from the start; they took Joe under their wing, made him laugh, made him part of the "in crowd," and watched him flourish and grow up. He has won many medals over the years, but more importantly, he found a soft place to land, a place where he could truly relate to others after his life-saving transplant at a young age. Joe also had the opportunity to show the world the power of organ donation when he rode the Donate Life Float in the 2015 Rose Parade in Pasadena, proudly holding Natalie's photo for all to see.

Joey as a toddler with Vic, already loving baseball.

Joey in Hillsborough Jr. Raiders Football & Hillsborough T-Ball, age 5.

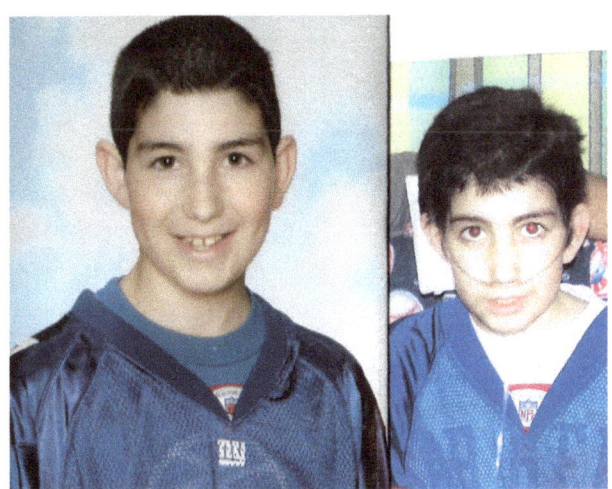

*Joey in 6th grade
- before transplant
and waiting for
transplant.*

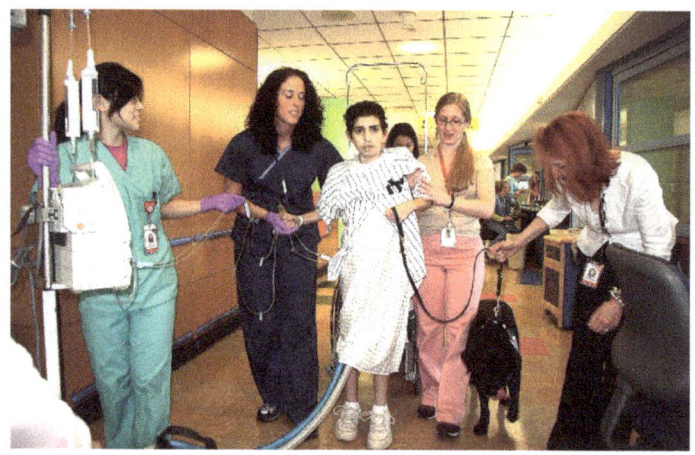

Joe taking steps in CHONY CICU with BiVAD heart machine, IV's, oxygen, therapists, nurses, and therapy dog.

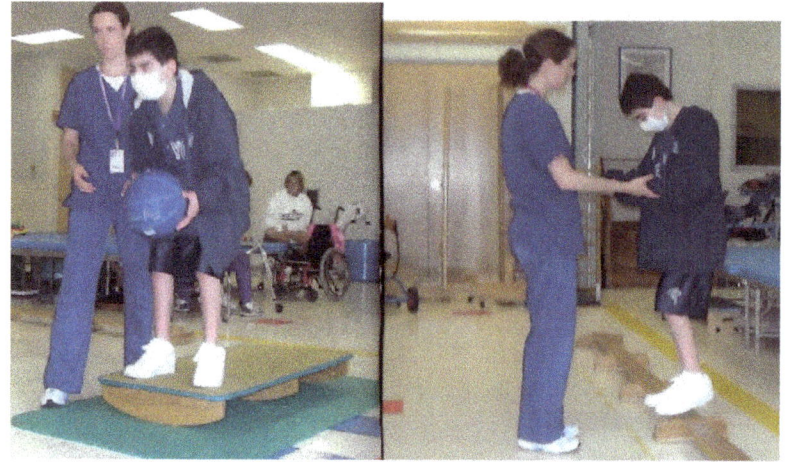

Joe doing rehab at Children's Specialized rehab hospital in New Jersey, 2006.

Laura and Joe with Mary Poppins in Disney 2008, Joe's Make A Wish Trip.

Patti, Victor, Laura, and Joe at a 2009 Bruce Springsteen concert.

Joe's organ donor,
Natalie (Naty).

Joe on the Donate Life Float
at the Rose Parade, 2015.

Joe meeting Guiliana, his donor's mom, at NJSN in 2012.

Joe on Team Liberty's basketball team, 2016 Transplant Games Cleveland.

Joe with his medal at 2018 SLC Transplant Games, with Laura and Patti.

*Patti and Victor volunteering at the 2021 Reimagined
Transplant Games, American Dream in New Jersey.*

*Patti receiving the 2022 Team
Manager Award at San Diego
Transplant Games from Bill Ryan.*

*Joe and Kacie's engagement
photo, 2022.*